"Reg Green has a powerful story of his own concerning the agony and the ecstasy that is the world of organ transplantation. But the strength of "The Gift that Heals: Stories of hope, renewal and transformation through organ and tissue donation," is that Green has presented us with a multitude of portraits -- reminding readers that the need is great, the choices painstaking, the rewards priceless. It is about everyday people and their confrontations at the confluence of life and death -- a most remarkable achievement." -- James Hill, managing editor, The Washington Post Writers Group.

"When Reg Green's son was murdered he might have been expected to retreat into grief; a bitter, diminished man condemned to a life haunted by the boy who was not there. Instead, he has worked tirelessly to promote organ donation.

This is a book about those who have received and given the gift of life and there is a golden light in it. Green has a skill with words and the journalist's knack for making a story compelling. The book is a celebration of life; of decency; of hope; of a little boy, and his father's commitment." -- Llewellyn King, syndicated columnist and PBS talk show host.

"Here are the faces behind organ donation: devastated families who, instead of turning inward in bitterness and despair, find the compassion to help others in desperate need, and organ recipients, who once at death's door, now run marathons, start families and resume their careers. Their stories, and those of the medical teams who make it all possible, are riveting." -- Robert Kiener, Reader's Digest.

"Reg Green probably knows as much as anybody on the planet about the rich, heartbreaking and transcendent realm of organ donation. He is also a fine, careful journalist and this combination makes this a most compelling and inspirational collection." -- Stephanie Salter, syndicated columnist.

The Gift that Heals

Stories of hope, renewal and transformation through organ and tissue donation

Reg Green

authorHOUSE®

AuthorHouse™
1663 Liberty Drive, Suite 200
Bloomington, IN 47403
www.authorhouse.com
Phone: 1-800-839-8640

First published by AuthorHouse   11/20/2007

ISBN: 978-1-4343-5068-8 (e)
ISBN: 978-1-4343-5069-5 (sc)

Printed in the United States of America
Bloomington, Indiana
This book is printed on acid-free paper.

Library of Congress Control Number: 2007908702

Contents

Preface

Close to half a million people in the United States have had an organ transplant. Millions have had a tissue transplant: skin, bone, corneas, heart valves, tendons. Yet, although transplantation is an everyday procedure in hundreds of hospitals around the world, public opinion still treats it as though it were on the fringe of medicine. Few people think about it at all until they become personally involved. It then takes over their lives.

The sobering fact is that any one of us could need a new organ or tissue to save our lives -- and virtually every one of us could be a donor.

Many people in this book are ordinary men, women and children who one day were told that unless someone donated a new heart or liver, kidney, lungs or pancreas they could not expect to live much longer. At that moment, they realized, perhaps for the first time, that someone else would have to die to give them the organ they needed.

Some of them had been sick all their lives, never knowing a normal day, going in and out of hospitals and aware that the end could come at any time. Others, including some world-class athletes, were seemingly in perfect health but were struck down without warning by a virus.

Some are people whose lives, though not threatened, were miserably constricted or in chronic pain: blind, suffering from severe burns and bent spines, unable to walk or pick up their children.

Into their world comes transplantation like a lifeline, some would say a miracle. It is not simply the best cure. For most of them it is the only cure. And because of the rapid advances in medical science, more and more people can benefit from it – sicker people, older people and people with more complex problems.

It is the most egalitarian of cures, leaping over all the normal social barriers. White men are walking around with black men's hearts inside them and vice versa. Asians are breathing through Hispanic lungs and vice versa. And -- dare I say it? -- Democrats see the world through Republican corneas and vice versa.

Transplantation is not a cure-all. As with any surgical procedure, complications of all sorts are possible, the powerful medications that recipients have to take so the body will not reject the new organ can have serious side effects and patients, who were sick enough to get to the top of the long waiting lists, have often developed other diseases that undermine their health, regardless of the revivifying effect of the new organ.

Even so, the results are astounding. However many times it happens, an inert organ, that has been taken from someone already dead, and springs suddenly into life in another dying body, still seems to most of us to have more in common with science fiction than regular medicine.

Success rates have generally advanced steadily year by year and dramatically over the decades. Results vary widely depending on the organ but, for example, about 95 percent of patients who have had a kidney transplant are alive after one year, 80 percent after five years and 60 percent after ten years. About 90 percent of heart patients are alive after one year, 75 percent after five years and 55 percent after ten. For lung patients the figures are 85 percent, 50 percent and 25 percent.

Given that all these people were terminally ill, that many were close to death at the time of their operation and that, over the years, some proportion of them will die from unrelated causes, the distance transplantation has come speaks for itself.

The waiting lists are the most obvious indicator of the distance it has still to go. The people on those lists live perpetually on the edge, always aware of a winner-takes-all race between a wasting disease and a cure over which they have no control. Every day 18 of them die. Nearly 100,000 people were waiting for an organ in the fall of 2007, compared with fewer than 20,000 twenty years earlier.

But even then, seen from another angle, those ever-lengthening lists are a measure of the progress of transplantation.

As techniques have improved across the board, demand for the procedure has skyrocketed, moving it in a few decades from experimental to common therapy.

The limiting factor, always, is the shortage of donated organs.

When all goes well patients who couldn't walk across the room without having to stop for breath are out of the hospital in a few days, back at work soon after, playing sports again. Athletes return to compete in the Olympics, win NBA championships and run marathons.

Generally, their whole life changes. They become rejuvenated, take up pursuits they have never had the energy for, have babies that were previously not even a possibility, climb mountains, get degrees and travel to faraway places. They relish even the most mundane routines – shopping, driving the car to work, being alone without worrying about a catastrophe.

As the stories in this book show, these people come from all walks of life, all temperaments and all philosophies. Some are deeply religious, seeing the hand of God in their own experience; some are intermittent worshippers, some firm non-believers – in fact, a cross-section of society.

A common thread, however, brings them all together. I am writing this book because my seven-year-old son, Nicholas, was shot in an attempted robbery while we were on vacation in Italy. A journalist who interviewed his seven recipients told us: "They are all very thankful to your wife and you and they think of you every day. But they speak of Nicholas in terms that I can only describe as reverence." So it is with recipients all over the world: they have their donor's photo in their wallet, send flowers to the family on birthdays, light candles and determine to be worthy of the gift they received.

The other people represented in this book are the ones who saved them. The great majority of donors never met the recipient and never will. They died and, in dying, their families, often acting on what their loved one had told them, agreed to make their gift without any knowledge of where it would go.

Donor families are as diverse as recipients. Some had scarcely heard of transplantation until suddenly faced with the death of one of their members. Others had talked about it freely. Some came to the decision agonizingly. For others it was so obvious they didn't even debate it. But all, at the moment when they were most vulnerable, instead of turning inward in bitterness and despair, set aside their grief long enough to help people they could only dimly imagine.

Some donors didn't die. Nowadays, an increasing number are living donors, who undergo a major and otherwise completely unnecessary operation, to give a kidney or, less often, part of their liver or lung, to help someone in need. Mostly that someone is a close relative and they regard the donation as a privilege. But at times it is a casual acquaintance or even a total stranger. When asked why they would put themselves at risk they typically shrug and say simply: "They needed it more than I did."

Despite all these differences, the power of transplantation has produced a response as strikingly uniform as that of recipients. Among all the hundreds of donor families I have met, I can scarcely remember one who regretted the decision. Almost all say it was the one good thing to come out of a terrible time.

It is those who didn't donate who often have regrets. At meetings about organ donation people will come up, with tears in their eyes, to say, "I wish I'd done that." Five, ten, sometimes twenty years earlier a family member had suffered brain death. No one approached them about donating or they were too upset to think about it or at the time the idea frightened them. Now they feel that somehow they let that loved one down.

Not that donation takes away the loneliness. More often than I like to remember, I will meet a young couple who say quietly something like this: "A few months ago our daughter's school had a presentation on transplantation. She told us that if anything happened to her she'd want to be a donor." They pause to pluck up courage and my heart sinks, knowing what is coming. "A few weeks later," they add, "she was killed coming home from school on her bicycle. We didn't hesitate."

People like that speak of the peace of mind the decision has brought them and the way it has helped them heal. "It's given a meaning to her death," they say. "It produced something good instead of everything being a waste."

In the absence of any previous discussion, a family in the waiting room of a trauma hospital is often bewildered. The circumstances of sudden death are always searing but, in addition, family opinion may be divided, some members who need to be consulted may be away, emotions can be running out of control.

Misconceptions are commonplace. Some people are convinced that if they sign a donor card the doctors will not try as hard to save them. Some think their church is against transplantation. Others say of someone who has just died, "I don't want her to be hurt anymore."

Everything is working against calm thought. A mother may have to call her husband at work to tell him their child was hit by a car. A father may have to tell his children their mother is not coming home.

Making a major, irrevocable decision there and then about something they have never seriously thought about is too much for many people. They say 'no' and often regret it for the rest of their lives.

The need is urgent because the potential supply is so limited. In the great majority of deaths, where the heart stops beating, the organs deteriorate too quickly to be transplanted. Most donated organs come from the small number of people, whose brain has stopped working and are truly dead, but who are on a ventilator that can keep their organs viable for a short time. By contrast, almost anyone can donate tissue – corneas to restore sight, skin to cure burns, bone to straighten spines, ligaments so that invalids can walk again.

A donation produces on average three or four organs, saving three or four families from devastation, in addition to tissue that can help up to 50 people. Most people in their whole lives will never again have as great an opportunity to change the world for the better as they have at that moment. With that much on the line, I often wonder what possible debate there can be about what is the right thing to do.

Life on the Waiting List

Shirley Coe's family carries a gene that attacks the heart with such persistence that three of her four brothers died young. The fourth was saved by a transplant. Several close relatives and many cousins have succumbed to it, some in childhood. Four other close relatives have had transplants. One of them, a niece, died when the donor heart failed, leaving a two-year-old son who was diagnosed at birth with the disease and has already had open heart surgery.

At 68, Shirley, who lives in Sandwich, Massachusetts, is the oldest living member of a very large family.

She herself suffered from the disease – hypertrophic cardiomyopathy, a thickening of the heart muscle that impedes the flow of blood – from her early 20s when she first began to be short of breath. During the birth of the Coes' first child more than 40 years ago, she went into congestive heart failure. For many years after that, she was fairly stable. But the last few years took a heavy toll.

She had irregular heartbeats and became accustomed to being hospitalized or taken to the emergency room to stabilize her condition. Gardening and walking even short distances became increasingly difficult. She was forced to retire early as a clinical social worker and almost gave up volunteer work. The restrictions were galling for a woman with so wide a range of interests.

"Many of my close relatives fell ill at a time when there were no defibrillators or pacemakers and medications were much less effective than they are today. At one time transplants were non-existent, then later rare and risky. Without that as a cure, they just died," she explains.

"In some ways, having this disease shaped our lives positively. We grew to appreciate every day. It didn't bring us down. It reminded us that to a large extent the quality of life is what you make it.

"Even so, you knew you could die without warning. You tried to put it out of your mind. But whenever another member of the family got sick, it came up in your face again.

"I have wonderful doctors and nurses, but they couldn't do anything more for me than they were doing. I was on all the medications that could help and in every case I was on the maximum dose."

Eventually, Shirley's medical team registered her on the transplant waiting list. "It's quite a traumatic event. You know you are there only because nothing else can save you. But you can see that to continue to live someone else is going to have to die. You think a lot of about life.

"You have to be strong enough overall to withstand the surgery, however, so when you go through all the testing and they put you on the list you feel relief and hope. 'I've made it,' you say to yourself.

"Then the wait begins. Your life is on hold. You can't make even short-term plans, let alone long-term ones. Hoping every moment for the call to come that tells you there's a heart for you is nerve-wracking. Sometimes, when I had a good day, I would feel I'd be content not to get better if I could just keep on going the way I felt then. But, if I had a bad day, all I wanted was to get on with it."

Sometimes the waiting seemed unbearable. "There are so few donor hearts available and they go to the sickest person first, as it should be. At times you feel you must 'crash' in order to be transplanted."

She gave the number of the cell phone that she carried wherever she went to only a few people but was so upset once, when a stranger dialed the number by mistake, that she reprogrammed it to ring in a distinctive way only if the heart unit at Brigham and Women's Hospital called. "That how on edge I was," she says.

Her husband, Dean, an executive recruiter, moved up and down on his own roller coaster of emotions. "There's a lot of anxiety in waiting, even though my life wasn't on the line like hers was. You turned a corner expecting to get to your destination and you saw nothing ahead of you.

"The tough part was when we weren't in sync, when one of us was having a good day and the other was overwhelmed. Then you'd both have to deny your own feelings to try to be supportive. At times when she was incapacitated, I didn't know whether to listen to her saying, 'I'm alright, it will pass' or call 911."

Although they have been married 45 years, the intensity of the experience has taught them new things about each other. "I'm continually surprised at her strength. Often she was the one who was supporting the rest of us," Dean says. "The longer this went on the more cohesive we became."

Hope blossomed, too, as they looked ahead. "You think of all the things you want to do that you can't do," Shirley says. "For years going up a hill was impossible. One of my first goals was to run in charity road races. Then I wanted to go kayaking with Dean. I wanted to get back into the work for the homeless. I wanted to garden and play more actively with my grandchildren."

Then one day the call came that she had hardly dared hope for and, despite setbacks from time to time, the results have been as liberating as she could have imagined. She cycles – "I hadn't biked since I was in grade school"–is back on the project for the homeless and is taking dancing lessons. Every morning when she wakes up, her first thought is, "What a wonderful day."

"All my life, I've lived within my limitations," she says. "Now I feel limitless."

A Race Against Time – Every Time

In St. Luke's Hospital of Kansas City, organ procurement teams were ready to remove the organs of a 25-year-old man who had been killed in a car accident. The most appropriate recipients had been identified and were already being prepared for their operations. Only the team that would recover the lungs was missing.

In one of the many heart-breaking upsets that can derail the finely-tuned transplantation process, the lung team called to say it was still in Indianapolis and the airport was closed by fog. A feverish debate about timing began. The heart and liver surgeons, already worried that they might lose everything, warned that they were running out of time. The only other airports from which a team might be sent were hours away. With heavy hearts, the decision was made to go ahead with the rest of the organs.

Rob Linderer, executive director of Midwest Transplant Network, describes what happened next. "This was too much to bear for Allison Hoffman, the transplant coordinator. 'This is someone's life we're dealing with,' she cried out. 'How can we throw away a perfect set of lungs?'

"The team agreed she could make one final desperate call and she made it to Barnes Hospital in St. Louis. 'If we can recover a set of lungs and get them to you in time, do you have a recipient?' she asked. 'Yes, we have,' was the reply. It was half the battle.

"But now she had another question. 'We don't have a lung program here,' she said, 'but will your lung surgeon accept them if our heart surgeon recovers them?' She knew this was a sticking point, it being very rare for heart or lung surgeons to let someone other than their own team recover an organ for transplant.

"As the two men talked on the phone to work out how the recovery could be done, Allison heard the answer to one of the most important questions she had ever asked in her professional life. 'They'll do it.'

"She and her colleague, Ryan Schmidt, who had minimal experience in lung preservation, then received directions over the telephone on how to preserve them for the journey."

Now all depended on how fast they could be taken to St. Louis. But here Midwest Transplant had an ace in the hole, its own twin-engine jet, a Citation CJ1, at the Charles Wheeler Downtown Kansas City Airport. As the ice chest and its life-saving cargo were rushed there, the plane was rolling into position, one engine already fired up. Even a few saved seconds were vital. A thunderstorm was coming in and in five minutes no more takeoffs would be allowed.

But those saved seconds made the difference. The plane lifted off just as the storm blew in. A little over an hour later the lungs were delivered to the operating room, where surgeons were waiting to place them in a 37-year-old mother of three young children.

Even in 25 years of doing this hairline work, this was one of the closest calls MTN's chief pilot, Dimitrios Roussopoulos, has had. He doesn't keep a running total of the times he has flown to deliver organs or take surgeons to operating rooms but he guesses it is around 6,000. "And every time, I still get a thrill knowing how much is at stake," he says.

Whenever he isn't flying, he has a pager and cell phone with him. He can't count the number of times the vibrator has gone off at the movies or baseball games. "I'm always happier when my seat is at the end of the row," he says.

As soon as the call comes in, he drops what he is doing and drives to the downtown airport. He files a flight plan, checks the weather, makes sure the plane is ready and then waits until the organs or the surgeons arrive. The moment they do, he and his co-pilot, John Jeffries, are on their way.

The plane, always kept in the hangar to make sure no time is lost in clearing it of snow or ice, taxis to the tarmac and is immediately directed by air traffic control to the front of the line. "We can save 20 minutes right there," says Dimitrios. "At airports in New York or Chicago it could be an hour."

With a top speed of 400 miles an hour, he quickly climbs to 18,000 feet. "Everyone is on instruments at that height. There are no amateurs up there," he says. "Mostly we fly at night and time is always pressing. You've got to be more alert than the average guy flying on a nice sunny day." Sometimes he goes 1,000 miles or more each way, but most of his trips are in the Midwest.

Often, as the plane lands at the other end, he can see an ambulance waiting in a special area, ready to hurry the ice chests or the surgeons on their way. If it's organs he's been carrying, he is soon on his way home. If the surgeons are doing a recovery, he waits, anywhere from three to six hours, depending on how many surgical teams are involved.

He fills in the time doing paperwork, watching television or walking around the airfield for exercise. It's essentially killing time until he has to jump into action again. But one essential factor is to check the plane once more. "Many people have the idea that pilots of small jets are happy-go-lucky types. We think of ourselves as being very methodical.

"It's true that things move so fast in the air that you have to react quickly. But you have to be patient enough to find out what's going on so you don't make stupid decisions. Pilots of private companies usually go for retraining every year. Airline pilots go every six months. We go every four months."

Coming home, when he has collected organs, is particularly rewarding. "I imagine the smile on the family's faces when they know we're in the air," he says. Once on the ground, he checks the aircraft yet again. "Making sure the plane is ready at all times can save minutes on the next trip."

Sometimes at a ceremony arranged by the organ procurement organization, someone he brought a heart or liver for will be pointed out to him. Not wanting to push himself forward, he rarely introduces himself. "But it does me good to look at them and know I played a part in getting them on their feet again."

"A Great Daddy"

Donna Banks, a features editor with Reader's Digest, then 39 years old, was talking on the telephone to her husband, Vincent, one October morning in 1992, when someone knocked at her office door. She looked up to see it was a messenger, said a couple of words and turned back to the phone. But by now Vincent didn't answer.

She'd been a little surprised at getting the call in the first place. It was true that he did have some good news: his work as finance director at the Children's Television Workshop had just been favorably reviewed and he was getting a raise. But he had already called her once that morning to tell her what presents he wanted to buy for their two boys for Christmas – a soccer ball for eight year-old Julian and a Tonka-type truck for Garrett, aged four. "It was so unlike him. We were always last-minute shoppers," Donna says. "Even then I wondered why he was already thinking about Christmas."

Now a great fear swept over her. She ran out of her office and asked her secretary to call his company, while keeping her own phone line open. She heard someone go into Vincent's room, then a bustle of activity as other people rushed in. They didn't know she was on the line but she could make out that they were giving him CPR and that it wasn't working.

"It was like a nightmare, hearing all those sounds and trying to piece them all together, imagining the worst but not really knowing how he was, shouting into the phone but not being able to make anyone hear," she says.

Urgently, her boss arranged for a car to drive her from her office in Pleasantville, N.Y. to St. Luke's-Roosevelt Hospital in New York City, where Vincent was being taken. But when she got there she was faced with another shattering experience: she was shown into a room where he was lying on a table, already dead.

"It was numbing. I found myself staring at a tag they had put on his toe. I knew they did that but I'd never seen it. That little tag summed it up for me: at 44, after 15 years of marriage, my husband and the father of our two boys would not be coming home."

That scene was the culmination of 16 months of anxiety which began, innocently enough, by Vincent finding himself a little short of breath when he lay down to sleep, though otherwise apparently in robust health. At first he thought it was something as commonplace as indigestion. Only at Donna's insistence did he finally see the family doctor, who did some routine tests.

"When the doctor called back, she said she wanted to see us immediately," Donna recalls. "I'd never had that happen to me before. As soon as I saw the expression on her face I knew that we were in big trouble, whatever this was."

It turned out to be cardiomyopathy, where the heart muscle is dying and for that, although medication could hold him for a while, the cure was a transplant. Meanwhile, in case they should miss the seriousness of the situation, the doctor told them Vincent was at risk of a heart attack or stroke.

As it happened, Donna had just finished editing an article on a man with cardiomyopathy, who had received a new heart. She knew the seriousness of what lay ahead. In January 1992, after the usual thorough medical and psychological testing, Vincent's doctors determined he was a good candidate for transplantation and registered him on the nation's transplant waiting list.

"I knew things could go either way: he could get a transplant and probably be fine or he could die at any time. For months the first thing I did when I woke up in the morning was to lie perfectly still with my eyes closed and listen to hear if he was still breathing."

What made the waiting harder was the warmth of the relationship between Vincent and his sons. She remembers him content with the most basic pleasures, taking them for bike rides or standing in his pajamas making pancakes for them and singing. "He was a great daddy," she says simply.

Now that he had lost the race against time, one decision was easy: when she was asked if she would donate his corneas, she unhesitatingly said yes. Although she has not met the recipients, she knows that two people had their sight restored.

It didn't stop the pain. "I learned that grief has a life of its own, which comes and goes when it feels like it. Sometimes I'd be driving to the supermarket, trying to decide what to buy, and I'd suddenly burst into tears," she says. "The worst part was that he was missing all those milestones – the first time Garrett scored a goal at soccer, the first time Julian made the lacrosse team."

Even in the early stages of his illness, Donna had started giving speeches on the need to increase donations. Bravely, after his death, she continued. "I never knew whether in the middle I might just break down. But my magazine has been covering transplantation for decades and I knew from my work there that personal stories are what make the difference when people are deciding whether to donate or not."

Close as she was to the subject, however, she was totally unprepared at the U.S. transplant games in Columbus, Ohio, for the masses of recipients marching, row after row, into the stadium, state flags flying, and being wildly cheered by a crowd that included families whose decisions had saved their lives.

"They were the picture of health," Donna says. "I cried uncontrollably. Not for the chance that Vinnie didn't have but for the chance all those people did have. It was a demonstration of human selflessness and it was awe-inspiring."

Grateful Husband Donates to Total Stranger

Dan Tomczak, a retired heavy equipment operator living in Darien Center, New York, steadfastly thinks of himself as an ordinary man. Yet what he wanted to do was so extraordinary in 2000 that the first two hospitals he consulted didn't know how it could be done.

Dan put himself in this position because of what at first appeared to be a minor problem with his wife, Ellie's, health. In 1983 she experienced swelling, especially in her legs. Her doctor advised her to buy elastic stockings and keep her feet up.

The swelling didn't go away, however, and she saw a series of doctors before a nephrologist gave her some good and bad news. "Your kidneys are scarred. Eventually you'll need a transplant. However, that's a long time ahead. In the meantime, just live a normal life."

Not being the kind to panic, this she did for another 15 years, working full-time, for most of those years as a clerk/receptionist at a dairy processing plant. By the end of that time, however, the symptoms had become much more unpleasant. "Every morning before I went to work I would throw up. Driving the 20 minutes home, I'd have to pull over to rest my eyes."

It was then she was told by her doctor, "You're getting close to having to go on dialysis – and we're putting you on the transplant waiting list." Only a few months after that and before she started dialysis, she answered the telephone at work. It was from the Erie County Medical Center and a voice said "This is *the* call." Characteristically, she stayed at work until the usual 5 o'clock and made sure things were shipshape for her replacement.

The next day the transplant operation was done without complications and four days later she went home. For years, despite the ups and downs that are not uncommon after a transplant, Ellie says, "It didn't hold me back from anything I wanted to do." But in time that changed. The transplanted kidney began to fail and she was put back on the waiting list, eventually getting a second transplant.

Meanwhile, Dan had come to an important decision. "Before the first transplant, it was very hard for me to go to work and leave her every morning in that state and not be able to do anything about it. When she got back home from work, that just about did her in for the day. I'd have given her one of my kidneys but we're different blood groups."

Now he felt he could do something. Two months after the first transplant he asked Ellie how she would feel if he donated a kidney to a stranger. "If that's what you want, I'll support you 100 percent," she replied.

That was the easy part. At that time fewer than 50 people had made a non-directed kidney donation. For months, Dan felt hemmed in by the understandable cautiousness of the health authorities. "You only need one kidney," he kept saying. "Many people are born with only one and never know it. I know there can be complications, but the risks seem low to me and I'm willing to take that chance."

To him it was obvious. "I saw what a transplant had done for Ellie. Why not do the same for someone else? I imagined someone out there, probably on dialysis, just waiting. I wanted to get on with it as quickly as possible."

Eventually, by going online and contacting other people who were donating a kidney to a family member, he got in touch with Thomas Jefferson University Hospital in Philadelphia. They agreed to do the operation when they found a suitable candidate.

It was still not cut and dried. One day he answered his cell phone to be told by the hospital, "We've got a bad result on your latest blood test. We don't know if we can use you." "It was like a knife through my heart," Dan remembers. The next test was normal, however, and in May 2002 he was called in and a kidney taken out to give to someone he still didn't know. Three days later he was discharged and says that with one kidney he has never had to forgo anything he wanted to do.

He was curious about his recipient but, having seen how difficult it had been for Ellie to write a thank you letter to her donor family, he didn't want to meet him right away. "I knew it would be emotional. I wanted him to become accustomed to his new kidney."

In Deerfield Beach, Florida, Michael Stern, a 6-foot, 4-inch salesman, then 53, was saying a fervent thank you. Things had not gone well for him since he left Philadelphia in 1999 to fulfill a 25-year-old dream to move south. Six months later, what at first felt like a sudden onset of flu had put him in the emergency room.

He felt so ill that when the nurse had finished examining him he could only say, "Please don't send me back to the waiting room." "You aren't going to the waiting room," she answered and that was the last thing he remembers until he woke up ten weeks later.

In the meantime, he was told, he'd suffered three strokes. "They paddled me back to life three times," he says. "But while that was going on, my kidneys went bad. I couldn't walk. When I got out of bed I fell to the floor."

He was put on dialysis and the transplant list. "It was then that I found out you don't just go out and get a new kidney." For a man who had always been active and ran every afternoon, struggling along in leg braces and being tied to a machine three days a week was agonizing. His spirits sank lower and lower.

At the dialysis clinic one day, his arm in a sling from falling down, his cell phone rang with a message. "This is Thomas Jefferson Hospital. I have a kidney for you." Twice on the way home he stopped the car on the shoulder of I-95 to hit the redial button. "Are you sure?" he asked. "Are you quite sure?" "Quite sure," said the nurse. "Go home and rest, drink a lot of water and don't stop on that interstate anymore."

A few days later Dan and Michael were on operating tables in adjoining rooms, though they never saw each other. "They told me it was a non-directed altruistic donation. I didn't know what they were talking about," Michael says. "When I found out, I couldn't believe it. I still can't fathom it. Even the doctors were blown away. 'This just doesn't happen,' they told me. And, do you know, he didn't want anyone to hear about it? There's no flash in him at all. He just wanted to be kind to the world."

A year later at a ceremony at Thomas Jefferson, Ellie, Dan and Michael met. "I'd imagined a big burly man," says Michael. "Instead he was small and wiry. 'I never pictured you like this,' he told me. 'And I never pictured you like that,' I said. But his heart is just as I imagined it. The transplant has totally changed me. I think it's made me a more understanding person. But Dan just goes on, doing good."

Now he has an 8x10 photo of the Tomczaks taped to the wall above his computer. "I want to be able to see them at any time," he says.

Dan has changed in one way. He has become convinced that telling his story will help others understand the importance of organ and tissue donation. He now shows the same determination in speaking at meetings and attending donor-card signing events as he did in making his own donation.

He has done one other thing: at 55, he retired from operating huge construction vehicles to do a two-year course in nursing. Now he works two 12-hour shifts a week at a nearby hospital, more if necessary. One good deed, it appears, however big, is not enough.

From Cancer Patient to Miss Utah

Jami Palmer grew up leading a country life in the tiny settlement of Park Valley in northwest Utah – helping out on her grandma's cattle ranch, hunting and going to a small elementary school where each teacher taught three grades – but from early childhood she set herself ambitious goals.

By the time she was 12 she was playing piano well enough to be preparing for a five-state competition and basketball in a team that made it to the regional championships. Almost every day after school she ran on the gravel road outside her house and practiced the long jump and had been taught by her brothers how not to throw a softball ball "like a girl."

"That's an exciting age – you're having your first crushes, starting to put on make-up, wanting to look beautiful – and all the dreams I had seemed possible," she remembers.

But one night, walking home from basketball practice, she noticed a bump just above her right knee. At first she thought she must have banged it during the game but, when she got home, she found to her surprise that it was hard. The family tried the usual home remedies – icing, heating and elevating the leg – but over the next few weeks, instead of going away, the lump grew. It was then that, for the first time, the word cancer came to her mind, though she dismissed it with the thought "Children don't get cancer."

She resisted going to the doctor, 100 miles away in Logan, until her parents, now quite anxious, insisted. When she got there, she assumed she'd be given a bottle of pills and sent home. Before the results of the tests she took were ready, she came home and played in the championship basketball game, which her team won, taking them to the regional tournament. Park Valley celebrated for days.

In Logan, however, the results were as bad as anyone had imagined and brought the celebrations to a dead stop. She remembers the drive, with her two brothers strangely quiet for the entire 100 miles.

She was sent to Primary Children's Medical Center in Salt Lake City for further evaluation. There she and her family received another shock. "You have a tumor the size of a softball and your femur is as fragile as an eggshell," they were told. "Bone cancer is very aggressive and moves very fast. You will have to start chemotherapy immediately and the treatment will last at least a year."

Her doctors found it hard to believe that the leg could have stood up to the pounding of playing for two basketball teams and the daily long jump practices. "You can't walk out of here," she was told. "If your leg breaks those cancer cells will be dispersed all over your body. From now on, until you're cured, you'll have to use crutches."

The hospital staff described the likely side effects: she would lose her hair and have watery eyes; she'd feel tired, lose her appetite and have mouth sores. Always, there would be the possibility of something much more serious, such as a stroke or heart attack. It was clear that she couldn't play any sports, wouldn't have the time to practice piano at a competitive level and wouldn't look beautiful. "It felt as though everything I wanted to do was lost," she says.

At the time she started her treatment, she says, the only source of strength she had outside her family was her membership of the Church of Jesus Christ of Latter-day Saints, the Mormon Church.

She was afraid of how her friends would think about her. Would she, who had been so active, now be a drag? Would they wonder if her cancer was contagious? She was very conscious of death. Cancer, she remembers, was much less talked about then and was still a source of shame. She had seen several victims in her own area. All of them had been drained by it and most had died. In her depression one thought kept recurring: "Why me?" For the first time in her life she felt embittered.

Some things helped. The road home from the hospital leaves the highway 19 miles from Park Valley and, as they traveled along it, deeply depressed, she began to notice paper plates attached to the reflector poles with writing on them. Her heart leapt when she saw they were messages for her. "Jami, we're there for you," "We're praying for you," "We miss you." And, finally, a word just being taken up by the local trend-setters, "Cool." Every quarter of a mile for the whole 19 miles the reassurances kept coming and, with them, her fears that she might not be accepted by her peers vanished. "They still think of me as part of the group," she thought.

The treatment lasted a year and a half and, by scheduling the sessions for Fridays, when her school was closed, and the weekend, she was back in the classroom on Tuesdays, maintaining throughout her A average.

As predicted, however, her hair fell out. An uncle shaved her head and she was fitted for a wig. She developed sores around her mouth. She felt washed out. And she missed her piano competition.

The tumor still had to be removed and her leg strengthened. In a procedure that lasted more than ten hours the tumor and tissue around it were cut away and ten inches of her femur removed. The tibia of a deceased donor took its place, buttressed by a 10 ½ inch titanium rod that was inserted through her hip.

Despite the novelty of the operation, it was "a tremendous success," Jami says. "I'm so grateful to the medical team and to the donor and his family. Without that combination of skill and generosity I could easily have lost my leg and maybe my life." She wrote a heartfelt letter to the wife of the donor, a 50-year-old man, describing how she had been rescued. "Having been in need of someone else's physical assistance makes you so thankful to people who put 'yes' on their driver's license," she says.

"'Why me?' gave way to the realization that I was one of the lucky ones. And with that realization I saw, too, that I could go after, not just the goals I had before, but higher ones."

She threw herself into the effort, exercising with such determination that in half the expected time she walked into the hospital without the crutches. "I wanted them to know I was resuming a normal life," she explains. At high school she went on to play for the varsity basketball and track teams, wrote for the school newspaper and was chosen junior prom queen. She took up the piano again. She graduated, earned a degree in communications at Brigham Young University and became a spokesperson with Make a Wish and the Musculoskeletal Transplant Foundation, the tissue bank. In 2007, she became deputy director of communications for the Governor of Utah.

"I also wanted to feel like a girl again. With cancer you don't feel very feminine," she says. "I was still self-conscious about the scar from the surgery, which runs from my ankle to my hip. At first I tried to cover it with heavy make-up. In time I realized, however, that was like covering up myself."

So she reached for a goal that, even before cancer, had never crossed her mind. In June 2000, on a glittering evening, buoyed up by the impassioned support of the 150 proud inhabitants of Park Valley, and in a pink dress that made no attempt to disguise the scar, Jami Palmer was crowned Miss Utah.

"It was a wonderful year, with the big hair and the rhinestones and the earrings and waving in parades and going on to the Miss America Pageant. But the best was going around seeing children in hospitals, knowing that my story could give them hope." She has changed, too. "I understand suffering much more than I ever did. You talk to these people, trying to help them, and you find it is they who teach you."

She estimates she has given 1,300 talks. The message is simple but powerful: "Set your goals as high as you can imagine. Even when things go wrong, life has a way of providing you with even greater opportunities. I did it. So can you."

It has captured hearts everywhere, like that of Maloree, a girl with leukemia whom Jami befriended and who, when the end was near, said she was not afraid and with only one wish would be content: "Please speak at my funeral"

Families Who Rise Above Grief

A pediatric emergency room is not a place for the squeamish. Children come in who ran in front of a car on the last day of school or fell off a bicycle or drowned while their parents went to answer the doorbell. These are not children who have suffered from a chronic illness where death could have been foreseen. The shock is total. "The parents hurt so much. Some of them seem to need help just to survive," says Mindy Zoll, a transplant coordinator.

Mindy has been with TransLife, the organ procurement group that covers 37 hospitals in central Florida, for 10 years, a lifetime where early burnout comes with the job.

She works solely with donor families. Once a year, at TransLife's remembrance ceremony, she will meet some of the recipients but has no ongoing contact with them. "I like to know who they are and how they are doing, but I want my focus to be entirely on the donor families. I don't want to make anyone feel compelled to donate or feel that they're wrong if they don't."

The work is full of stress. "We have 10 request coordinators and, at any one time, four of us are on call, 24 hours at a stretch," she explains. "Even when we're not on call, we wear a beeper so that, if there's a sudden rush of cases, they can get us right away. I've done as many as five requests for donation in one day and at five different hospitals.

"When a call comes in, it's from a hospital where there is a potential organ donor, someone already declared dead or, at times, a patient whose family has decided to withdraw life support when there is no hope of recovery.

"I get all the preliminary information I can: where the patient is, how old they are, what happened to them and, if possible, some medical history. I also want to know about the family: where they are, are they coming in? Sometimes we don't even know who the person is, let alone their family. Then we have to dig deeper.

"I drop whatever I'm doing and drive to the hospital. I always have my scrubs and gear in the car so I'm ready to go. When I get there I read the patient's chart and talk to the nurses to find out as much as I can about what happened. Then I meet the family and take them to a place where we can talk.

"That's the first time I've seen them. They are a rainbow of society and all in the grip of strong emotions – shock, anger, regret, guilt, fear.

"Many are stunned. Over and over we hear people ask 'why me?' Or 'it was too soon' or 'it's not fair.' They can't find the good in it. For their peace of mind they need to work their way through this. I don't give them answers. I just support them while they figure out how they feel. I try to find out what they've been told and sort out any misconceptions.

"Many of them are angry with someone – a mother, perhaps, with her divorced husband because their son was in his care when he drowned or a family with the hospital because it couldn't save their child or just because they think it didn't communicate with them well enough.

"Most families don't deal a lot with death, so they don't know about death certificates or funeral arrangements or about the medical examiner or if there's going to be an autopsy. And they are so hard hit they don't even care. We answer a lot of questions and explain the little things they can't fathom so they can concentrate on what they really need to do, which is to be with each other and try to grasp what's happening. And while they're doing that we need to make sure they aren't hungry or sleep-deprived or overrun with people who want their signatures.

"But I also need them to understand brain death. Sometimes the nurses will say, 'Oh, yes, they understand that' and I'll talk to them and find they don't understand at all. What I need to hear from them is that they know he's dead and won't be coming back. That tells me they understand. But if they say things like, 'There's very little hope,' or 'We want to have him transferred to another hospital,' I know they aren't there yet. Sometimes I have to break off for a while because I can see they're still hoping he'll get better.

"I tailor what I say to what I hear them say to me. Some of them need a clinical explanation. Others just can't handle that and then I use common everyday language. Even then, some families just don't believe it. Maybe someone has made a mistake in their case before and, with something as important as this, they feel they can't afford to take a chance. In those cases I often ask them if they'd like to witness a test, where the patient is taken off the ventilator, and let them see for themselves that he isn't breathing.

"A few families want something more and then I may ask the physician to show them a cerebral blood flow study, which is a moving x-ray of blood flowing to the brain. First they see what a normal one looks like. The blood is very bright. Then they look at the one for their loved one and all that's there is a dark void.

"It's very painful for them to watch these tests. No one wants them to be true. But it helps them to believe and they need to believe before they can go on to grieve and accept.

"Whichever way they come to it, once I'm sure they understand brain death, I tell them about organ donation – what the process is and why it's needed. I'm careful not to make them feel guilty if they decide not to, but I do tell them that there are families waiting and hoping someone will make that choice.

"When I started doing this work 10 years ago, most people were surprised when I talked about organ donation. It was a new idea to them. Now more and more of them know what it means. Many of them have thought of it only in passing, figuring it wouldn't ever apply to them, but at least it's a step forward.

"When I do introduce the subject, there's a whole realm of reactions, all the way from gratitude and relief to anger and fear and, in some families, all of them together. Many, of course, can hardly take it in. Some are so numbed that they can't even string words together. Often they cry while trying to decide. And often, too, especially when it's children, I cry along with them.

"Even when they've agreed to donate, it's hard to say goodbye, particularly when it's children. Many families won't go home until we've gone into surgery. The mother of one child even waited outside the surgery until we finished almost three hours later. She couldn't leave until she knew everything was over.

"But, however difficult it is at the time, I've never met one family of the several hundred I've worked with who afterward has said they were sorry they donated, not one.

"The number one reason why people say yes is they feel that, if they could ask their loved one, that's what he would say. And, in some cases, he actually did say it. That's why telling your family your wishes and signing a donor card or putting your name on a statewide donor registry is so important.

"Many others just want to make something good out of a tragic situation. I remember a construction worker who had an accident at work. He'd led such a good life and his family was so proud of him. They wanted something good to come from his death just the way good had come from his life."

Once the family has given its consent she goes online, connects to the computer system operated by United Network for Organ Sharing, enters information about the new donor and runs a "match list" for each organ. That information -- including age, height, weight, blood type, cause of death and physical condition of the organs -- identifies patients registered on the national transplant waiting list who are biologically compatible with the donor. Potential recipients for each of the organs are listed in order of priority, depending mainly on how sick they are but also on how close they are to the donor hospital and how well they are expected to do with a transplant.

The organs are first offered to the matching patients in local transplant hospitals, then regionally and, finally, nationally. "I contact the transplant hospitals where each of the patients is registered," Mindy explains. "I tell them I have, say, a liver offer for such and such a patient and they will tell me if that person is available for a transplant.

"Sometimes they aren't available. They may have become too ill to withstand the operation or perhaps the hospital is so busy that all the surgeons are already out on cases. Or maybe the patient is traveling and can't get back in time. Miami might say no if they have a hurricane coming through. New York may be having a blizzard.

"In time I'll have worked through the lists and the transplant centers will have accepted all the organs. Then I need to set a time when their surgical teams can get together in the operating room at whichever hospital the donor patient is in. The transplant center taking the heart may be in Atlanta. Perhaps the one coming for the liver is in Jacksonville.

"I find the team that is furthest away and ask them when they can be here. They may say three hours. Perhaps it's now 11 o'clock at night. That fixes what we call our OR time for 2 a.m. I call all the transplant centers again to tell them the starting time and we begin our own preparations, including more telephoning.

"If all goes well, by 2 o'clock all the teams should have arrived, in each case a surgeon and one or two assistants. The operating room is crowded, with 15 or 20 people, and very noisy. The team taking the heart goes first, because the length of time it is viable outside the body is the shortest. The rule of thumb is five hours. After that it's the lungs, then the liver, small intestine and pancreas and, finally, the kidneys, which can be transplanted up to two days later. When everything is being recovered we're in there for about five hours.

"At first the atmosphere is quite relaxed. When we take the patient, already deceased, into surgery they are on a ventilator so the heart is beating and blood is being supplied to the organs. The teams can do quite a bit of surgery at that stage, just as they would if they were operating on a live patient. There comes a point in the middle of the surgery, however, called cross-clamp time, when they clamp off the major arteries. The heart and then the blood flow stop and the countdown starts for the time they have to recover and transplant the organs into the recipient. Everything suddenly becomes very hectic.

"When we cross clamp we begin to flush the organs with a cold preservative solution. They are packed for transport in this solution in sterile insulated containers to keep them as cold as possible to minimize damage to the cells. The warmer the cells are, the quicker they die -- though we mustn't freeze them either. Then the race is on to get them into the recipients just as quickly as they possibly can.

"The first surgeon will take the heart and he's gone, already on the roof and into the helicopter or in an ambulance, with the lights and sirens going, while the others are still working. One by one each team leaves and, in the end, it's just two or three people cleaning up, and everything is quiet again.

"I generally help put the patient in a shroud before they are taken to the morgue and I always thank them for what they gave. I think of their family at home, in a house that suddenly seems empty, and I want them to feel that I cared for their loved one, just like I would my own."

Mother's Persistence Revives Life-Saving Procedure

When Susan McVey Dillon, of Downingtown, Pennsylvania, received a call at work one Friday afternoon in June 1995, telling her that her 14-year-old son Michael had fallen off a rope swing and had been taken to the local Brandywine hospital with a head injury, she was anxious but not unduly alarmed. Michael was a bundle of energy who, she always said, went to bed simply to get recharged for the next day. Falls were a part of his life, false alarms common.

But her blood froze when a social worker was waiting for her at the hospital door. "I'd been in that hospital before. They'd never treated me like this," she says.

"Michael is in the operating room with a severe head trauma. He has a blood clot in his brain," she was told. No, she couldn't go in to see him. But, yes, they would keep her informed of all developments. She

30

understood they were doing everything they could but knowing so little was torture. She called her divorced husband, Mick, who immediately set out for the hospital, and other members of her family, several of whom came, too.

It happened that, at the time of the shift change, two trauma surgeons were on duty, one of them a well-known local surgeon, the other the chief neurosurgeon from Walter Reed Army Medical Center. "'That's where they take the president,' I found myself thinking. I felt that I was in good hands," Sue remembers. Both doctors stayed on the case all weekend.

From time to time, small pieces of information came out from behind the closed doors, each time deflating the small hopes that had built up in the meantime. The blood clot had been removed but now that didn't seem to be the main problem. Michael's cranial pressure was very high and was resisting all attempts to bring it down. He couldn't breathe without a respirator. His temperature was 108.

"I was just learning what most of this meant. But you don't have to have a medical degree to know what a temperature like that can do to the brain," Sue says. "I think I knew then that Michael was not likely to get out of that bed and come home. I realized that we might soon have to make some important decisions."

Though her mind was in turmoil, she was beginning to think about organ donation. "I always felt that if one of my children needed a new kidney to stay alive, I'd expect one to be available. So, if another child needed a kidney to stay alive and I could provide one, how could I do anything else?"

The thought was easier to bear because only a few months before when Sue's daughter, Janette, got her driver's license the family had had a perfunctory talk about donation. Michael reacted with the matter-of-factness of youth. "If my organs can help someone else, why not? I wouldn't need them."

By now Sue had learned that Michael had minimal brain stem activity, the pressure on his brain was still inordinately high and it was extremely unlikely that he would ever be able to breathe without a respirator. "We asked every question we could think of. And then we asked more," she says. "We wanted to know what if this? What if that? Are there radical treatments you can try? The doctors answered everything, very patiently, but all the time whittling down our options until it came down to this: he might die, but, if he didn't, all we could do was keep him on life support indefinitely or, more likely, until he got pneumonia or one of his organs began to fail. But he would never have a meaningful life again."

Sue thought of another Pennsylvanian, Karen Ann Quinlan, who was on life support for 10 years. "I know we all have different opinions but I always felt it was very unfair for her to have to go through that. I couldn't believe Michael would have made that choice for himself."

With the family in agreement, she asked to speak to someone about withdrawing life support and then donating Michael's organs. The call was referred to John Edwards, clinical administrator of the Gift of Life Donor Program, based in Philadelphia.

For him it was something quite new. He had handled 30 or 40 cases of deceased donors and knew of a few programs around the United States where patients, who did not meet the criteria for brain death, had been taken off life support once their care was deemed futile. A small number of these patients had become organ and tissue donors. There was even a term for it: donation after cardiac death, or DCD.

Gift of Life hadn't done a case for many years, however. Among other things, it requires a finding by the medical team that the patient's injury is non-recoverable and a family that has already decided to withdraw support.

It was not a new departure, however. In the early days, this is how all organ donations had occurred. However, with the adoption of criteria that established brain death, DCD donation fell into disuse in the 1980s.

In brain death, the organs function normally until they are recovered, because they are maintained by a ventilator. In DCD cases, the ventilator is turned off and organ recovery does not occur until the patient dies. As the heart rate slows and the blood pressure drops, the organs receive less and less oxygen and can deteriorate.

For DCD patients, the recovery teams are obliged to work even faster than normal to keep the organs as viable as possible. The heart and lungs, being more susceptible to the interruption of blood supply, are the most difficult to recover.

Gift of Life was able to carry out the family's wishes. Recipients, who were perfect matches for the kidneys and liver, were identified through United Network for Organ Sharing's computer-based system for matching donated organs to candidates on the waiting list. The corneas also were placed.

Seeing the benefits so clearly, Sue went on to start a campaign for donation after cardiac death, challenging hospitals and organ procurement groups to review their procedures to accommodate as many cases as possible.

In time she was helped by the greater willingness of families to consider end-of-life decisions. Removal of life support is now routinely done in hospitals throughout the United States for those with non-recoverable injuries, whether organ donation is being considered or not.

The campaign became the nucleus for a program at Gift of Life that has resulted in 300 donors, for a total of 600 transplanted organs. Gift of Life also has helped train organ procurement organizations across the United States in this type of donation. Says CEO Howard Nathan, "At one time we didn't do it at all. Now it is a routine element of our program. It was through Sue's persistence that it all started."

The Lung Recipient Who Ran a Marathon

Six years ago Len Geiger's lungs were so bad that he couldn't walk and talk at the same time. Three years ago he completed a marathon. And he did it side by side with the father of the girl who saved his life

Through his late twenties and early thirties, Len, an area sales manager for a pharmaceutical company, blamed his shortness of breath on the pack of cigarettes a day he used to smoke. If not that it was lack of exercise, he told himself, and made a mental note to do something about it – some day.

Periodic bouts of bronchitis jarred him enough to see a doctor, who gave him an expectorant, antibiotics and instructions to go home to bed. But none of that brought more than temporary relief.

The turning point came on his birthday when, having had dinner with his parents, he was unable to walk across the parking lot with them to their car. "Here I was, at 35, in front of my mother and father, leaning on a stranger's car and gasping for breath." He shudders at the memory.

The next morning his doctor, as baffled as he was, sent away a sample of blood to test for an ailment he believed Len didn't have: Alpha-1, genetic emphysema. The test came back positive. There was no joy in finally nailing the cause. "It's progressive, irreversible and ultimately terminal," he heard the doctor say. "We might be able to slow it down, but we can't cure it."

The symptoms, in fact, got worse. "Not only didn't I like climbing stairs, I couldn't climb them," Len says. Even to get through a normal day, he was forced to carry a bottle of liquid oxygen at all times. In 1996, he went on disability. In 1997, his doctors put him on the transplant waiting list.

Meanwhile, the steroids he was taking to keep down the inflammation in his lungs attacked his hip bones. "Walking, indeed almost any exercise, was agonizing." In early 2000, both hips were replaced. "It was a godsend compared to what it had been before, though it was awkward and I learned there was no possibility that I would ever be able to run properly again."

His lungs were steadily deteriorating. "There was a sense of terror about doing anything, a feeling of drowning and gasping for air. I was afraid to do something as simple as go to a football game: it was so painful just to walk from the car to my seat. I felt ashamed when people looked at me, shuffling along like an old man."

Eight years passed and, for long stretches of time, Len scarcely thought about the transplant. "It seemed so remote and the difficulty of just getting about dominated my thoughts. Every now and then, however, it would hit me how scary it all was."

Then one Sunday afternoon, his cell phone rang in his home in Gainesville, Georgia. A nurse was saying, "We have lungs for you." A few hours later he was in the operating room at the University of Virginia Medical Center in Charlottesville.

He heard a voice say, "The doctor has approved the lungs." The next morning he woke up with those lungs inside him. Four days later, on a treadmill, he was walking at a pace of four miles an hour and the physiotherapist had to tell him to slow down.

"I could scarcely believe the difference. Breathing was enjoyable again," he remembers. "Before, every breath had to be forced in and then forced out. It took me weeks before I was able to relax and just let it happen."

Everything pointed to a complete recovery. But less than three months later, he was back in an emergency room – this time from a quite different cause. Wanting to regain strength as quickly as possible and unable to run, he had bought a mountain bike. Pushing the speed on a single track trail through the woods, his front wheel caught in the bushes and threw him over the handlebars, breaking his leg in five places. The first doctor to examine him said, "I don't know if you'll ever walk again."

Nevertheless, the Gainesville surgeons did more than he could have hoped for, aligning the leg with a series of steel plates. All seemed to be going well until, without warning, he suddenly stopped breathing. He was revived but put on life support and placed in a drug-induced coma. For three weeks he hung between life and death.

At last he came to and gradually recovered enough strength to go home.

He now had something else on his mind. All he knew of his donor was the cold description: young female. For months he tried to write a letter that LifeNet Health, the organ procurement organization in

Virginia, would forward to her family. "I couldn't get something down on paper that I felt comfortable with. I think it was mainly because I was trying to tell my whole life story and express all my feelings," he explains.

"Then a friend said to me, 'Just say thank you.' And that's what I did: a year after my transplant, a one-page letter that simply told them how grateful I was." Three months later, he got a reply and a photograph. His donor was Korinne Shroyer of Lynchburg, Virginia, 14 years old, a soccer player, dancer, singer and member of the school band, who had dreamed of becoming a model. "It was hard for me to comprehend how I could be alive and such an active, talented and vivacious girl like that dead."

Korinne's parents, Kristie and Kevin, and their younger daughter, Kolby, have had to find their way every day through what must be one of the most searing experiences imaginable for a family. Until a few months before her death, Korinne had been a happy, outgoing child. But then she began to have mood swings -- intensely happy at times, deeply depressed at others. She told her parents what was happening and how mystified she was by the change. "We worried that it might be more than the normal pains of adolescence, so we took her to a doctor, who suggested an anti-depressant drug," her father, Kevin, says. "Ten days later she shot herself."

For six days she was in a coma. But almost from the start the doctors told her parents she had only a 10 percent chance of survival. "After two days, Kristie and I agreed that we had to sit down and talk about what to do if she didn't survive," Kevin recalls. "It was very easy for us to decide she should be an organ donor. We both knew that if she could have woken up, she would have said, 'Mom, Dad, that's what I want you to do.' That's the kind of person she was. Of course, we never stopped willing for her to recover. But, if she had to die, we didn't want her to die in vain."

He still can't get used to the thought that he won't see her graduate from college or have children or that all her photos stop at age 14. But five people were saved by her organs and the pain felt by many others has been reduced by Korinne's corneas, bone and skin. One of the recipients wrote an anonymous thank you letter but the Shroyers have not heard from any of the others, except Len Geiger. Yet that has produced results none of them could have foreseen.

The two families arranged to meet, doing so dramatically in front of television cameras to draw attention to the transformation organ donation can achieve. Kevin, the investigator for the public defender in Lynchburg, Virginia, is a dedicated runner. Almost without discussion the two men, both in their mid-forties, agreed to take part in the eight kilometer race organized every year by LifeNet, in tandem with a marathon.

In November 2003, 15 months after he broke his leg, and with titanium and ceramic hips preventing anything like a real run, Len loped, speed-walked and fought his way over the five long miles with Kevin at his side every step of the way. "I think Len wanted to prove to everyone, including himself, that he could do anything a fit, healthy person with the proper training can do," Kevin says.

The resulting publicity for organ donation cheered them both and they made plans to do it again the next year. Later, however, Len began to think that a rerun would be an anticlimax. He called Kevin and said: "Let's do the marathon."

Although by then Len had run in triathlons and two half marathons, Kevin worried that this was too big a leap. "That's twice as far as you've ever run in your life," he pointed out. "Remember how much you were hurting at the end of that first half marathon." But he was wasting his breath.

In November 2004, throwing out first one leg, and then the other, and dragging the trailing leg behind, in what he calls 'power walking,' but must be one of the most ungainly ways of doing the race since its origins in 490 BC, Len, with Kevin at his shoulder, began a race whose severity is beyond the imagination of even most healthy people.

Having to hold back his own pace was hard on Kevin, too. "I couldn't stretch my legs in the way I normally run. Occasionally I'd run ahead a block or two and then run back to him. But mostly we were next to each other. It was a very emotional thing for us both.

"By the time we were at the 18-mile mark he was in serious, serious pain. I watched him forcing himself along and I finally said 'Look, Len, if it's hurting that bad we could stop here and get some help. You've done more than anyone could ever have expected.' He wouldn't hear of it. He took a couple of anti-inflammatory pills and after that he never complained."

In the end, the two men crossed the finishing line, hand in hand, arms raised, in 6 hours 25 minutes and 17 seconds. Once again, the publicity for organ donation was gratifying, including coverage by network television.

"It was excruciating," Len remembers, "and I can't believe I'll ever do it again. But I did it and I did it for the right reasons. All this could only happen because Korinne's parents not only gave her organs but had the generosity of spirit to make a friend of me too." In return, when the Geigers had a daughter, they called her Ava Corinne.

As for Kevin, he says he savored every moment. "That's as close as I will ever again come to running with my daughter."

The Transplant Surgeon Who Needed a Transplant

Dr. Daniel Hayes, director of transplantation at Carolinas Medical Center in Charlotte, North Carolina, loves his work. During more than 20 years, he has performed some 900 kidney, liver and pancreas transplants. He is still awed when he looks at a patient on the operating table and sees only an empty space where the liver used to be, and thrilled when a donated liver, cold, pale and drained of blood, is put into that space and within minutes starts functioning.

Or when a new pancreas has just been transplanted into a diabetic, who has been dependent on insulin shots to keep him alive, and the anesthesiologist announces quietly, "He's making insulin." It is technically exacting work, requiring close attention to detail. "Some of the vessels we have to sew together are small and, if we don't do it right, blood will spurt out all over the place," he says.

"You also have to be very careful when you remove an organ. The liver is always diseased, perhaps swollen and misshapen. The normal blood-clotting parameters don't apply. Many patients have had previous surgeries, so there's a lot of scarring that you have to watch out for. A mistake at that stage can be disastrous."

So Hayes was shocked professionally, as well as personally, when in 2000, aged 45, his eyesight suddenly began to deteriorate. "At 16, I had been diagnosed with a mild case of keratoconus, a condition where, because the cornea isn't a smooth curve, light is not directed accurately on to the retina. For the next 30 years, wearing glasses had taken care of the problem. Now the shape of my corneas was changing abruptly.

"I started to wear hard contact lenses, the only kind that corrected the keratoconus, and then, as the deterioration progressed, I needed both glasses and contacts all the time. But even that was not enough. Within a few months, I went from short-sightedness to seriously-impaired vision. Objects a few yards away looked fuzzy and I couldn't see anything at a distance."

All this time, however, he continued performing transplant operations that could last up to eight hours. "Luckily, I was able to see well close up and, with the telescopic instruments we use, I did dozens of transplants.

"But the hard contacts were beginning to irritate my eyes. If I had an operation to do one day, I'd come home early on the afternoon before and take them out. When I was on call, I did the same thing. I could live with that but I began to worry that it might not be long before I couldn't wear the contacts at all. And without contacts, I could scarcely see a thing."

The time had come, he decided, to have a transplant. In November 2003, he was given a new cornea in the right eye. He waited nine months for healing to occur and then had a transplant in the left eye.

Even before the second operation, he was doing organ transplants. "I was euphoric at getting back into the operating room," he says. "I could already see so much better."

But it was only after the second transplant that he moved to a level he'd never known. "For the first time since childhood, I had perfect vision. I drive at night without worrying about having to read the street signs. I can fish, golf and water ski -- things that had been on hold for years. And, of course, I can do my job.

"If people think of transplantation at all, it's usually about saving lives through the major organs. Doing that kind of work myself, that's what I normally think of. But tissue donation can enhance lives dramatically, too."

"Baby" of the Family Saves Four

Just before 1 o'clock in the morning on Mother's Day 2000, Jessie and Frank Ginoza, both retired, were startled by the telephone ringing in their Honolulu home. It was a friend of their 28-year-old son, Steven, scarcely able to speak, telling them that Steven was in the emergency room at Queen's Medical Center with a severe head injury. Frank rushed there but Jessie, though consumed with fear, had to remain at home to take care of three of their young grandchildren who were staying with them.

When Frank arrived, the news was worse than he had feared. Steven, celebrating with some friends after the end of their last volleyball game of the season, had been riding the rails of the escalator in the Ala Moana shopping mall and had fallen 20 feet to the floor. It was clear that he couldn't be expected to live. The news had spread quickly and 20 of his friends were already at the hospital.

Frank went home to be with Jessie, then back to Queen's again. "I felt I had to be near him," he says. "It gave me just a little hope." But soon even that hope was extinguished and Steven was declared dead. By then Jessie had arranged for the grandchildren to be looked after and was at the hospital, too. A coordinator from the Organ Donor Center of Hawaii came to ask them if they would consider donating his organs.

"I felt sure he would have wanted that. He was in the bone marrow program and had often given blood," Jessie says. "The hardest thing was that his two sisters were away. Steven was the baby of the family and, in a way, he was their baby as much as ours. And now they wouldn't even be able to see him one last time.

"One of my friends who came with me was appalled. 'How can people be so insensitive to approach you when you're beside yourself with grief? How can they even think of asking you?' I remember crying a lot and trying to explain to her."

Frank and Jessie, still at the hospital, were told that Steven's body needed to be medically stabilized so his organs could be used for transplant. Even now, Frank smiles sadly, remembering that, where before he had been praying for his son to recover and come home, now his hopes were fixed only on him getting to the point where the donation could take place. Both parents stayed on until Steven, now stabilized, was taken into the operating room where his organs were recovered. Then, in the evening, they drove home to a house where, to this day, their son's room has been barely touched.

Sometime during that long day, Jessie's friend took her to one side. "I didn't understand how quickly it had to be done and how many people could be helped," she said. "I've learned a very valuable lesson today."

At a service attended by 800 people, including Steven's teachers from grade school on, the Methodist pastor at his college said that Steven had been a bridge between himself and the other students. It's an image Jessie and Frank see as the symbol of both his life and death.

Four people's lives were saved. One recipient is the head coordinator of the Minority Organ and Tissue Transplant Education Program, who works mostly with the Filipino population of Hawaii. Another became vice-president of the Transplant Association of Hawaii. The recipients' families have grown. As honored guests, the Ginozas have attended first birthday parties and graduation parties of families they had never known before. As Jessie says, "Steven's donation has multiplied far beyond what we could ever have expected."

Liver Recipient Becomes Olympic Medalist

Chris Klug stood at the top of a steep, icy, windswept slope in the high mountains above Park City, Utah, facing the biggest challenge of his career as a snowboarder. In the first run for the bronze medal in the parallel giant slalom of the 2002 Winter Olympics, he had finished four hundredths of a second ahead of his rival, Nicolas Huet of France. Now the second and final run was about to start.

The last few minutes had been dismaying. On the first run a buckle on his boot had snapped and all the hectic efforts of the team technician to repair it had failed. "My foot was loose in the boot. I couldn't pressure properly or feel the snow," he remembers. "For a 50-cent piece of plastic I could lose this race, I thought. Then, with seconds to spare, the coach dug into his bag and produced a pipe fastener. I couldn't believe it. But he cinched that on the boot, gave it a final twist, added a few wraps of duct tape and said 'That will have to do. Good luck, Chris.'"

The starter was looking at his watch as Chris shot up to the start and, bang, they were off, hurtling 40 miles an hour down a 35-degree slope on a board measuring 85 inches by 10. Halfway down, and in front, he felt a smile crease his face. "I've got this race," he thought, then instantly wiped out the idea. "Focus, focus," he told himself. "Don't celebrate yet."

Forty-five seconds from the start, he flew past the finishing line, turned around to see Huet just coming through the last gate and was engulfed in a sea of wildly cheering fans. He had the bronze. But more than that, he had just become the first medalist in Olympic history to have had an organ transplant.

The moment had been a long time coming. Growing up on the mountain slopes in Colorado and Oregon, he was skiing almost as soon as he walked and the Olympic dream seemed less of a fantasy than it does to most children. By the time he was ten he had discovered snowboarding. "That was the end of my skiing career," he says. "I was hooked."

At first the sport was on the fringes: there were no major competitions, no circuit and no thought of it becoming an Olympic event. But in the years that followed all that changed and Chris, a natural, began to work his way up the competition ladder. Right after high school he was on the World Cup circuit, training round the clock and competing every weekend around the world. By now snowboarding was even beginning to be seriously considered for Olympic competition.

Then came the first cloud in this bright sky. "In 1991, when I was 22, I took a routine physical and my liver enzymes came back strangely high. I was baffled. I felt like a million bucks. My first thought was that whoever did the tests was nuts.

"But over the next year or so, after a zillion blood tests and biopsies and consultations, it turned out he wasn't nuts. I had something called primary sclerosing cholangitis, which I found out was a disease that constantly scars and re-scars the bile ducts, constricting and eventually closing them.

"All this time, however, I was competing on the World Cup circuit, traveling to Europe and Asia, living the dream. I still couldn't take the warning signs seriously, not even when one of my doctors told me 'One day you'll need a transplant. It could be one year or five or 20. But one day it will be necessary.' Okay, I thought. So I'll come back in 20 years and by that time they'll probably have figured something else out. So I went on training and competing and racking up national championships. I found it hard to think that I was a sick man."

To his doctors it was serious enough for them to have him evaluated for a liver transplant. While on the transplant waiting list, he had a procedure done each year to open the bile ducts. But to him it remained more of an irritating diversion than a major part of his life, which was a preparation for his first Olympics, 1998 in Nagano, Japan.

"I had a good debut there. After my first run I was in the silver medal position. It was within my grasp. But my second run wasn't good enough and I finished sixth. It was a big disappointment. From then on 2002 was always on my mind.

"Snowboarding is a unique sport. You need to have so many different qualities --strength, stamina, coordination -- and you have to keep training regularly to stay on top. So, besides snowboarding, I'd ride single-track trails on my mountain bike around Aspen, practice for hours on my skateboard, surf and have long workouts in the gym.

Occasionally, I'd get an infection and take antibiotics, but it was nothing out of the ordinary."

In 2000, seven years after being told he would need a transplant and six years after going on the waiting list, he was again the U.S. National Champion.

Only a few months later, however, the situation had changed dramatically. Relaxing after his championship win, he suffered from a bout of what seemed like 'flu but wouldn't go away. "One night I woke up feeling as though someone had stuck a dagger in me just where my liver was. I was scared to death and realized the time had come."

At the University of Colorado Hospital in Denver, the urgency was quickly confirmed. The bile ducts were so tightly closed that the physicians could hardly open them, even temporarily. "They said I needed a new liver without delay. On the transplant wait list that would probably take three or four months. But no one knew if I could last that long.

"At first I tried to keep active and not lose too much weight. I went for rides on my bike, worked out in the gym and ate sensibly. But within a few weeks that was too much for me. I gradually scaled back, then more and more, until even after a game of golf I'd come home utterly exhausted and have to lie down for the rest of the day.

"It was the hardest thing I've ever gone through. For the first time in my life I felt my health wasn't in my own hands. You realize you have no control over the future, you're just hanging on. When I looked at myself in the mirror I could see a yellow and weak old man. After two months I was beginning to give up hope." At last, in July 2000, the call came through. Chris' supportive family and girlfriend, Missy April, flew with him to the hospital in Denver. "By then I was fighting for my life," he says.

But next morning the operation went without a hitch. In three weeks he was on light exercise and in seven weeks back training with the U.S. team. Six months after his transplant, he won a World Cup race.

Since then he has cut his daily dosage of immunosuppressants from four milligrams a day to one and has never had an episode of rejection or infection. He says he listens to his body a little more than he used to, taking care not to overdo things. "But apart from that I'm healthier and stronger than I've ever been."

He has set up the Chris Klug Foundation which, among other things, spreads awareness of the need for organ donation in high schools and colleges, through a program called Donor Dudes, in the sports he loves best: surfing, skateboarding and snowboarding. Most of all, by his story alone, he has proved to tens of thousands of people that transplantation can restore life to the very peak of human fitness.

Nurse Dispels Myths about Transplantation

Although Charlette Thompson has looked after cardiac patients in intensive care units in Lexington, Kentucky, hospitals since the 1980s, she has never become accustomed to sudden death. After all these years there is shock in her voice when she describes it. "They'd be looking at you, talking to you, and the next second, the very next second, they'd be gone."

Charlette went into the ICU by choice. "I wanted to take care of the sickest patients," she says. "But seeing so many deaths made me want to do more than keeping the dying comfortable."

About that time, Kentucky Organ Donor Affiliates (KODA) was looking for nurses, and especially African-American nurses like Charlette, to do voluntary work outside their normal jobs to help raise donation rates in a region where, even by the standards of the time, they were very low.

"I could see how difficult it was," she says. "Most people at that time, black or white, knew almost nothing about organ donation and most of those who did know something were afraid of it. Some thought they needed all their body parts intact when they went to heaven. Many said, 'If I sign my license they won't even try to save me.'

"Often someone would say to me, 'There's no point in doing it. It doesn't work anyway.' Black people mistrusted the whole thing. 'All those organs go to the whites,' they'd say. And they'd add: 'My church is against it.'"

A devout churchgoer all her life, she knew that wasn't so and decided to hit the problem head on. "The only way to reach black people in large numbers was through the churches," she says. She began contacting pastors all over the area and asking them to give her just 10 minutes to talk. She set out to dispel the myths surrounding transplantation.

"When I first went in, I'd ask how many people knew anything about it," she says. "Always it was almost zero. And when I asked who was in favor, it was the same. So I'd talk about how so many black people were dying because of the shortage of organs. I'd tell them that their church was for it. I'd talk to them about people I knew who were alive because of a transplant. In just that few minutes, people were nodding their heads and, at the end, when I'd ask, almost all would say they agreed."

But she knew a lot of work was needed if this was to be more than good intentions. She encouraged KODA to train more minority requestors, spoke at forums, worked on literature for minorities and helped set up the African-American Task Force on Organ Donation to create awareness of the donor shortage.

In 1995 she contacted Dr. Clive Callender, one of the few African-American transplant surgeons in the United States, and asked him to talk at the biggest church in the area, Shiloh Baptist Church. His visit was electrifying. "People came away saying, 'Transplants do work and they do help blacks,'" Charlette says. "And to hear it from a famous surgeon who did these operations and was black himself, that blew their minds."

She was often asked as a volunteer to approach families who had just lost someone to see if they would donate. "When I'd go into a hospital where an extended family had gathered it was often noisy, sometimes chaotic. With all those people there it was hard to come to an agreement. Often they were angry with me. 'Why are you coming at this time?' some of them would ask, not knowing that it had to be done then or not at all.

"Often it was young people who'd been killed in a car accident or maybe there'd been a shooting. I'd say 'Before we do anything, let's pray.' I wanted to calm everyone down. Then perhaps I'd ask, 'What sort of a person was he? Was he a giving person?' Often they'd say, 'Oh, yes, yes, that's just what he was like. He was always helping others.' And right then, without me saying another word, they'd see that he could still give. Sometimes I'd ask them if they'd like to sing a hymn and we'd sing quietly among ourselves before we ever talked about donation.

"Sometimes just one voice would have everyone in doubt. I'd try to find the strongest ones in the family and I'd make a point of making sure they understood. From then on they would often take over from me. You could never be sure. You might go in there, thinking it was the older family members who'd be against it, but sometimes it was the grandmother who made everyone see it was the right thing to do."

Of all the letters sent to Charlette by people who decided to donate, she says there has never been a negative one. "Even those family members who were doubtful at the time, when they hear of the joy they have brought to the family who got the organs, they say, 'Now I'm sure -- that's what he would have wanted.'" A colleague who watched her in these situations explains her successes succinctly: "She puts everyone at ease."

Then, seven years ago, in her early 40s, her active life hit a barrier. She developed a brain tumor and, after two operations, lost 90 percent of her vision. She had to give up nursing. She could read only by closing one eye and using a powerful magnifying glass. It tore at her that she had all that knowledge and experience and yet was unable to help. "I gave a few speeches and went to meetings from time to time. But it wasn't enough."

Then one day, calling on her faith, she began to write a musical play. "I've been a gospel singer all my life and I had a group called Charlette's Web, but I'd never done anything like this before." Slowly and painfully, supported by her husband, Richard, and two grown daughters, she wrote "Be Careful of the Stones You Throw," about two friends, African-American girls, one of whom needs a transplant. It was shown first to a full house at the Opera House in Lexington and then at the Singletary Center for the Arts.

"It made converts all over the area," Jenny Miller Jones, director of education at KODA, reports. "It was typical of her that, finding it impossible to save lives one way, she found another."

But then her own life became easier, too. To her great joy, her sight has improved so much that she can drive again. And, fulfilling a long-held wish, she has become an ordained minister.

Coach's Tissue Lets Others Play the Games He Loved

Mike Craig of Newark, Ohio, aged 51, loved sports. A 6-foot 4-inch 230-pound high school science teacher, he coached basketball, track and, his greatest love, football at Johnstown High. Almost every evening of the school year, he was with his students. On Fridays and Saturdays there were the games and, on Sundays, films.

One of the football players was his own son, Chris, who played quarterback and safety. They saw a lot of each other – in the classroom, on the field and at home. In June 2003, when Chris graduated, it was Mike who gave him his diploma and a proud hug.

On Sunday morning two weeks later, Mike said a few cheerful words to his wife, Gail, and stepped outside his home to fix a problem with the air conditioner. A few minutes later she heard him calling her, though so faintly she could hardly believe it was him. She opened the door to find him slumped there and could see he had crawled from where he had been working.

She remembers crying out over and over, "Mike, what's wrong, what's wrong?" She fumbled with the telephone and called 911 and then, with the operator talking her through the steps, tried frantically to resuscitate him. "But he was so big – and so stiff – I could hardly even get him turned over," she says with a shudder. She was down on the ground, still pounding his chest, when the ambulance arrived and put him on a defibrillator.

Her 16-year-old daughter, Molly, happened to come home immediately afterward with her best friend and all three watched with mounting horror. But nothing could save him. Mike had been electrocuted and only his exceptional willpower and strength had enabled him to move so far.

At St. Ann's Hospital, in Westerville, 25 minutes away, a chaplain confirmed to Gail that he was dead. Soon after that she spoke on the phone, through what seemed like a fog, to a transplant coordinator from Lifeline of Ohio. As his heart had stopped beating, she couldn't donate his organs but she could, if she wished, donate tissue.

Gail, a medical transcriptionist, knew about organ donation. "We'd always put 'yes' on our driver's licenses. But I had no idea what tissue they could use or how much of it or even what some of it was. But then the transplant coordinator said, 'You know, a lot of it could be used to heal sports injuries' and I knew for sure it was what he would have wanted." She quickly said yes and Mike's eyes, heart valves, bone, skin, ligaments and tendons were recovered.

Meanwhile, Gail's world was getting smaller and smaller. Five weeks after Mike died, Chris left home to go to Wooster College and joined the football squad there, with his mother traveling to see him play as she always had.

At one game she talked to the parents of Chris' friend and teammate, Mike Vyrostek, who had torn a ligament the week before. "He's had three previous injuries, and they've used all they can of his own tissue," they told her. They were uneasy because the doctors were planning to use the tissue of a deceased donor. "They just didn't feel comfortable," Gail says.

She worried about it herself and then made up her mind. She called Lifeline and asked if any of Mike's tissue was still available. The group had never done a directed tissue donation before but they could see how important it was to her. They discovered in a series of phone calls that some of the tissue was still being stored and they arranged for a piece that could be used on young Mike's leg to be sent to Ohio.

That piece has repaired the injury so well that he says it has healed better than any of the other three operations that used his own tissue. "Mike was very close to the children. It makes me feel better to know that every game a little bit of him is down on the football field with Chris," Gail says.

Molly also is now away at college and Gail's house, recently bursting with exuberant young life, is very quiet.

Two years after Mike died, Whitney, the friend who was with Molly that day, was killed in a car accident. As soon as she heard the news, Gail went to see Whitney's mother, who immediately asked her a question that took her breath away: "I need you to tell me. Is it okay if I donate her tissue? I don't want them to hurt her." Gail didn't have the slightest doubt. "Yes," she said, "It's what's keeping me going."

Parishioner's Heart Saves Her Pastor

The pain that Father Dalton Downs felt in his upper abdomen during the late nights was discomforting enough for him to seek medical assistance. But tests showed it wasn't ulcers or hiatal hernia and nothing else seemed to be wrong with him. For a man who had had virtually no illnesses all his life and was the very active pastor of St. Timothy's Episcopal Church in the south-eastern segment of Washington, D.C., the only medical advice he got that seemed to him to be on target was "just cut back on the spicy foods you love."

In late January 1994, however, the symptoms, including sweating, headache and shortness of breath, occurred for the first time during the day. His wife, Ana Jo, took that as a serious warning and, despite her husband's protests, called 911. "When I got to the local hospital they treated me as if I was in the midst of a heart attack. I was astonished," he says.

"Four days later the results of all the tests were in and they were negative -- namely, that I did not have a heart attack. Yet it was more than making a big deal out of an upset stomach."

He was referred to a heart specialist who, unable to identify any problem with the heart, recommended a sonogram. Within minutes of the procedure, Dalton was shocked to find the room he was in had suddenly filled up with doctors and nurses. "There's the problem: transposition of the main arteries," he heard one of them say. "And you say that he is 58 years old?" another replied. "He's not supposed to be alive."

It turned out that, despite his energetic life, he had been functioning with a deformed heart. "From today you have to cut down on 85 percent of the things you do," he was told. "You're in a stressful job that goes from one crisis to another. You have to give up your athletic activities: no more tennis, soccer or scuba diving."

Further tests brought the kind of announcement all patients dread. "I have some very bad news for you," the chief cardiologist told him. "Your heart is so destroyed that I can't explain how you are still walking around."

Then, worse still. "I don't think there's anything we can do for you, except put you on medications to keep you as comfortable as possible." It was nothing less than a death sentence.

He and Ana Jo sat in stunned silence, too downcast to talk, until at length he asked, "Isn't there anything we can try?" The cardiologist paused a moment then said, "There's only one other thing. We can see if you qualify for a heart transplant. But it's a long shot and the waiting list moves very slowly."

On Mother's Day 1994, Father Downs, who was on sabbatical leave, went into the pulpit of St. Timothy's Church and told a tearful congregation the whole story. "There's nothing you can do about it," he said, "except to pray for me and my family. However, there is something you can do to help others like me. Share the gift of life. Become involved in promoting organ donation."

At the end of the service the first person out of the pews was Dawn Alexander, a close friend, who was in charge of the nursery school program. Tears streamed down her cheeks as she embraced him. "I feel your pain," she said. "I just want you to know that if I had two hearts I would give one to you right now."

A year followed with no sign of the precious heart. By now, Dalton's weight was down to 114 from 178 pounds. One Sunday morning, while he was celebrating the Eucharist, brought another blow: an urgent message that he was needed at Greater Southeast Community Hospital. Dawn Alexander, 38 years old, was in a coma. It turned out to be a cerebral aneurysm and she never regained consciousness.

That could have been the final scene but it wasn't. Months before, unknown to Dalton, Dawn had told her family, "If anything happens to me and Father Downs is still looking for a heart, I want him to have mine." After a discussion, they agreed to respect her wishes, although it all seemed only the remotest possibility.

For two days after Dawn fell ill, until the end, Dalton ministered to the family at the hospital. On the afternoon of the third day, he got a call from his cardiologist at Georgetown University Hospital, who said: "I'm calling about the lady from your church who died this morning. Do you know that she left you her heart?" For him the surprise and conflict of emotions – gratitude mixed with grief, relief with pain -- were almost overpowering.

A few hours later at the hospital, the doctor told him, "Everything matches. We will have the transplant operation tonight." As far as he knows, it was the first directed heart transplant outside a family anywhere in the world. Nine days later he was discharged.

Messages of support flooded in. Among them was one from Archbishop Desmond Tutu, who called him from South Africa the second day after the surgery and told him, "Don't try to talk. I want to let you know that we are sending out your story to our churches and asking for their continual prayers for you. This is indeed a powerful message of hope."

On the second Sunday of September 1995, Father Downs was back in the pulpit at St. Timothy's Parish. The church was packed -- not just with the congregation, but also with friends and the news media. "There was a lot of joy and a lot of tears," he remembers.

"During the Passing of the Peace, I saw Shae, Dawn's nine-year-old daughter, in the distance. She came running up to me and said, 'Father Downs, peace to you. I love you. May I listen to my Mommy's heart beat?' And in the silence of the sanctuary, she placed her ear against my chest. It was one of the most precious moments of my life."

Since then St. Timothy's Church has thrown itself into the campaign to increase organ and tissue donation. It was the first church to become a member of the Minority Organ and Tissue Transplant Education Program (MOTTEP), the group that promotes awareness of the donor shortage among minorities.

Born in Nicaragua and with close ties to both the Latino and black population of Washington, Father Downs speaks to interested groups of all kinds, promoting organ and tissue donor awareness and addressing their fears and concerns. "God has entrusted your life to you," he says to them. "You live in a house and when you do not need that house any more you can give part of it to someone else to fix up their own house."

At 71, he says he has the kind of medical problems "that come with age," but he adds, "The heart is working great." So is his spirit.

After 1,000 Transplant Operations, Surgeon Still "In Awe" over Results

On the day, early in her career, that Dr. Velma Scantlebury was offered a position working with Dr. Tom Starzl, one of the most venerated physicians in the transplant field, she walked back to her car and, making sure no one was watching, jumped into the air and clicked her heels.

The first African-American female transplant surgeon, and now professor of surgery and director of transplantation at the University of South Alabama Regional Transplant Center, she still feels that way about her work. After performing more than 1,000 kidney transplants, she says, "I'm still in awe - especially when we've just put a new kidney into a patient, who has been dependent on a machine, and see that kidney work even before I leave the operating room.

"It's hard to convey the thrill of seeing something as basic as a transplanted organ making urine, something that the body has not been able to do for itself for years. Within days, the patient will probably be leaving the hospital."

Treating children brings out special problems. "When I first see them they often can't eat enough or hold on to substances enough to gain weight or grow. As the disease takes over their body, it's important to perform the transplant before the brain starts to suffer the consequences of organ failure." Because the risk of developmental delay is high for children not transplanted, pediatric patients get preference in the allocation system.

Patients of all ages frequently surprise her. "When they come back for a regular check-up, the change is remarkable: there's color in their skin, they've often gone back to work and their spirits are high. When it comes to children, you often can't recognize the tiny, pathetic creatures who came into your office a year or so before."

Patients she has treated as young teenagers or adults will often come back with children of their own. "You feel like a grandmother to them," she says.

After-care has its own rewards. "We have a lifetime relationship with them. Some surgeons in other fields meet their patients, perform the operation and then it's goodbye unless something goes wrong. In transplantation, you monitor them for the rest of their lives. A lot of our work is managing the drugs they must take to be sure they don't develop side effects that, in some cases, can be as disabling as the original disease.

"Even so, we have to remind them that this organ is foreign to their body. Our job is to prevent acute and chronic rejection and make that kidney last as long as we possibly can. Otherwise, they will go right back on the waiting list."

She gives special attention to teenagers. "Years of illness have often made them much smaller than their peers and they are very sensitive about being different. They very much want to be like everyone else. If they feel the medications are distorting their physical appearance or making them abnormal, there is a great temptation to skip doses. It's one of the most troubling aspects of dealing with teenagers."

This kind of interaction builds close relationships. "We get to know each other so well that transplant patients are very quick to tell any new hospital staff who did their operation. After many years, and even after moving to a different area, they feel they have a security blanket. They can always pick up the phone and call."

As for the operations themselves, every one is different, she points out. "Transplantation involves so many judgment calls that, when I come out of the operating room, I'm drained mentally rather than physically."

Timing is crucial, so there is always pressure to make sure that everything comes together as it should. "Living donor kidneys can be scheduled with some degree of certainty but deceased donor kidneys become available without warning and normally arrive at the airport late in the day. We're always concerned whether they'll get here in time or if they'll match the description we've been given. Then they have to be examined to make sure they match the intended recipient."

Even then, something can go wrong. "Sometimes the patients don't tell us they've had an infection or maybe a blood transfusion recently and suddenly all the matching we've been doing is nullified. Or sometimes a kidney is smaller than expected and not suitable for the large man or woman we had in mind. Sometimes it will be too badly damaged for us to use.

"So, when we call patients to tell them there is a match, we always say there's a chance the kidney we are getting might not be suitable for them. But they come in with such high hopes that it's heartbreaking for them – and for us, too – when we have to tell them, 'this one won't do for you.'"

Unlike livers, on which Scantlebury was first trained, kidney patients have the alternative of dialysis to keep them going. But it is a hard life and some of her patients have had to deal with it for ten years or more. "These machines aren't as good as a naturally-functioning kidney, so over time there's a build-up of substances in the blood. At some point, too, most of the blood is out of the patient's body and with all that fluid going in and out there can be a lot of blood pressure problems. When their session is over, many patients can barely make it home and get into bed.

"It's not surprising. The machine has just taken off ten pounds of fluid they've accumulated since their last session. Some patients can still work full-time and continue dialysis three evenings a week at the clinic. But very few do. Dialysis keeps people alive but it's a big price to pay."

Still, when life is at stake, things fall into place. Scantlebury is still surprised that when cases have gone badly, with multiple problems, a rejected organ and the patients having had to spend a long time in the hospital, how often they say, "I know that if it goes well a transplant can change my life. I want to try again."

Engulfed by Fire, Saved by Donated Skin

About 5 o'clock in the evening on October 21, 1996, the Glendale, California, fire department was dispatched urgently to try to contain a brush fire in a highly flammable canyon in Malibu, ringed by several hundred homes. They set up their equipment on the side of a hill, laying out the hoses, wetting down the hillside and watching warily an inferno that seemed to stretch almost to the ocean.

At that time, the winds were blowing offshore and, after spraying the houses and checking that all the occupants had left, the firefighters took turns to make sure no embers blew their way. They slept all night in the street with their helmets as pillows.

All seemed to be going well until, at about noon the next day, the wind suddenly changed direction, heading straight for a section manned by the crew of Engine #24. "The fire was down in the canyon below us, when suddenly a gust of wind caught the flames. Before you could snap your fingers, it was on us," recalls Bill Jensen, one of the team, who had been with the department 28 years. "Our captain shouted at us to drop our hoses and run. We didn't even turn them off. All I could see was a solid orange wall of flame. It knocked me to the ground and blew me against a wall."

When the flames passed, Bill got to his feet and staggered to the road. His protective clothing had disintegrated in the intense heat, skin was hanging off almost every part of him and he was grotesquely swollen. He had lost his goggles and a glove, the plastic on his belt had melted into his waistband and ashes from his uniform had penetrated his burns. More than 70 percent of his body was covered in second- and third-degree burns. The paramedics doused him and drove him a mile or so to where a helicopter could land. He was taken to the UCLA Medical Center, where he was stabilized, and then transferred to Grossman Burn Center in nearby Sherman Oaks.

At home his wife, Sue, was watching the fire on television. Reports came in that six firefighters were injured, including a 28-year veteran. "I knew right away it was him," she says.

At the burn center, Bill was put into a drug-induced coma so that he could be treated. The doctors, he was told later, gave him a five to 10 percent chance of living. "The key in cases like this is to remove the dead skin as quickly as possible so that, as it breaks up, the body doesn't carry it to the kidneys and clog them up. That's how you lose patients," says Dr. Richard Grossman, director of the center.

"We remove the devitalized skin and cover the raw area with donated skin. That stops the pain and keeps out the bacteria that would otherwise grow and multiply. This avoids changing dressings twice a day, which is quite painful. In a smaller burn, after five or six days, we remove the donated skin and take skin grafts from the patient's body and place it on the healthy bed," he explains.

"With Bill it was different. With this massive burn, we would return every five to seven days, remove the old donated skin, clear up any devitalized tissue we didn't get and put on new donated skin. This went on until we had a healthy bed and could take his own skin and put that on. Eventually, all that thin skin, which at first looked like wet tissue paper, became his new skin, allowing him to heal and keep out bacteria."

But in this case nothing was simple. "We had so few places where we could go where he wasn't burned, mainly the bottom of his feet, his chest and the top of his head, that we had to use much more skin from deceased donors than usual. We did that by faking his immune system, giving him anti-rejection medication, so that his body wouldn't recognize that it was not his own skin."

It's a far cry from the simple wet dressings or antibiotic soaks that burn centers used to use, hoping that the skin would regenerate naturally, or even the pigskin that was widely used in the 1970s as a temporary substitute for donor skin. "Pigskin is very much like human skin. It saved a lot of lives but it was often rejected in a week or ten days. Many times the burn surgeon had to replace it with new pigskin until the wound was ready," Grossman says.

"Even now, human skin, like donated blood, is always scarce," he adds. "That's why donating tissue is so vital. One donor can help so many people. It's a multiple endowment." On average, his center alone does six or seven operations a day on burn victims.

For Bill's badly burned face, Grossman used a special instrument, a high-speed sander that removes the dead skin and smoothes out the surface. "It operates at 20,000 revolutions a minute, but is remarkably gentle on the features. Obviously, we don't want to do anything that would add to the damage." Donated skin was then laid on top and, later, grafts of his own skin.

Some parts, like forehead and cheeks, were so deeply burned, however, that they had to be cut away before the new skin could be laid on. In effect, the whole left side of his face and the right cheek are new. For Bill, the sander was one of the most painful parts of the entire process. But the skin looks smooth, his naturally florid complexion has been preserved and it is difficult for a casual observer to notice any abnormality.

His left hand, which was so badly burned that it resembled a skeleton, presented the biggest challenge of all. By a process that Bill still recounts with awe, the team made two incisions in the skin around his stomach, making a pocket under the skin, then sewing up the hand inside it to keep it sterile. "He looked like Napoleon," says Grossman.

There, it began to grow granulation tissue on the knuckles and tops of the fingers. Three weeks later, the pocket was opened and an object that Bill scarcely recognized was brought out and covered with donor skin.

"They trimmed that down to the size of my hand and divided it into fingers and then put skin from a deceased donor over it. Then, step by step, as they could take a piece of my own skin from some place on my body, they would put it over one finger, then another."

"He doesn't have a lot of function in that hand but it's viable -- a world of difference from being amputated," Grossman comments, who adapted the technique from one pioneered during the Battle of Britain, when fighter pilots were often hideously burned.

Altogether, Bill has had more than 100 blood transfusions and huge amounts of donated skin grafts. "Some of it was brown skin, some yellow, some black," he says. "I owe my life to the world."

After his discharge, he still had problems. Both his lungs and kidneys suffered damage and he is susceptible to pneumonia. "I slept in my La-Z-Boy chair for almost two years because I couldn't lie completely flat. Even now the skin is so thin in some areas that if I just rub against something it can open up." But his spirits are high and he seems to have avoided the psychological damage that afflicts so many people who have been badly burned.

The Malibu/Calabasas Incident, as it came to be known, made Bill and his team famous. No lives were lost and, of the hundreds of houses at risk, only three were destroyed. In time all the other members of his crew went back to work. Now, as a member of the Firefighters Quest for Burn Survivors, he is a vigorous advocate for tissue donation and safety measures to protect against burns, especially for children. "He's like a one-man visiting nurses association but he does it all quietly and out of the limelight," Grossman comments.

For a burn victim, his greatest wish while he was in the hospital may seem strange: to sit by his own fireplace. His summing up is equally surprising. "This was one of the best things that ever happened to me. It made me realize that everything in life is important. I don't care whether it's rain or sunshine. I enjoy every minute of the day."

Transplant Team Copes with Child's Tragedy Amid World-Shaking Event

At 10 p.m. on September 10, 2001, Bruce Zalneraitis, then clinical director of Life Alaska Donor Services, was called to Alaska Regional Hospital in Anchorage to help with a tragic case. A 13-year-old boy, Will Dean, had just shot himself in the head and seemed likely to die at any time.

When Bruce arrived, the emergency room team was still giving the boy large quantities of fluid and blood products to replace the blood lost from the wound and had placed intravenous drips in both arms. But it soon became clear that not only could they not save him but also that, in his highly unstable condition, they would have a difficult time just keeping his heart beating.

Will's mother and father, Jill and Tim, are divorced – and at the time she was in Saipan and had to be reached by telephone -- but when told their son was a candidate to be a donor both said they were in favor. It was something they had discussed while they were still married. It seemed fitting that a boy known for his patient and gentle touch with small children and pets should at the end still be helping others.

At 2:30 a.m., no brain activity could be discerned and Will was given the full range of tests to put all doubts to rest. Bright lights were shone into his eyes and sharp pins were used to prick his arms. He was given a gag test and taken off the ventilator for 10 minutes to see if he would breathe spontaneously. There was no response to these or any other tests and at 3 a.m. he was officially declared dead.

By 5 a.m., Bruce was telling his organ donation colleagues at LifeCenter Northwest in Seattle, the organ procurement organization that covers Alaska, that potentially seven organs and two corneas had just become available from a boy weighing 140 pounds and blood type O-positive. At their end, the Seattle team accessed United Network for Organ Sharing's computer system to match the donated organs to the sickest candidates with the best genetic matches.

Once the organs were allocated, calls were put in to book the two corporate jets that are always kept on standby at Boeing Field to take the specialist surgeons to the hospital where the donor was. The long distances between Alaska and anywhere make time even more critical than elsewhere. For livers, kidneys and pancreas, timing is always a concern but for hearts and lungs everything has to go right. Bad weather or even a slight mechanical problem can unravel the donation and everyone's hopes.

Arrangements are dovetailed to save seconds. While the planes are in the air, bringing the transplant surgeons, the organ procurement team is providing them with updated information about the donor. When they are on their way back, the crews are reporting progress to their own hospital: "30 minutes out, 15 minutes out, we're in the ambulance." Even before they land, the operation on the heart and lung recipients is under way – their chests are opened and the lines are in. In Bruce's words, "the recipient is placed on the bypass pump when the surgeon comes through the OR door carrying the heart in the ice chest."

On the day of Will's donation, the donor team at Anchorage was doing its part, maintaining the oxygen supply and blood pressure and reducing the dependence on drugs, to make sure the organs were working as normally as possible. But at around 5 a.m. they were interrupted by a nurse who came in to say that a terrible accident had happened in New York.

It was four hours later on the East Coast on the morning of September 11 and a plane had just crashed into the north tower of the World Trade Center. Two hours later, word reached Bruce that the FAA, acting on orders from the military, had grounded all civil aircraft in the United States.

The schedule put together with such speed would have to be scrapped and, with it, the donation itself. Among the confusion and disbelief of that day, Bruce still remembers the special pain he felt hearing that news. "Here we were, witnessing the enormity of one of the worst things that has ever happened to this country and yet struggling, in a small way, to bring some good out of the terrible loss of a child," he says.

"We decided that, even if we couldn't move Will's organs by air, we would at least take his kidneys to Seattle by van, because they can last longest outside the body. It's 2,300 miles but we would have saved something."

A hectic series of phone calls from Alaska and the clinical director of LifeCenter Northwest followed and, in the end, the FAA granted a special exemption for the jets to fly. At 6 p.m. they took off from

Seattle into eerily empty skies – the first civilian planes, Life Alaska was told, allowed to fly in all American airspace since that morning.

At 9:15 p.m., the surgeons were in the operating room in Anchorage. At 12:22 a.m., the cross clamp went on and Will's blood stopped flowing. Minutes later, his heart and lungs were removed and the first team left, while the second team continued its work to remove the other organs.

Twenty minutes later, the first team was in the air and all was going well. As they approached Seattle in the black of night, however, fighter planes that had apparently not been informed of the exemption intercepted them, declined to accept their explanation and forced them to land at Bellingham, Washington, close to the Canadian border.

There they were surrounded but, to their great relief, quickly established their identity. But now another worry took over. They were 90 miles from the University of Washington Medical Center and already dangerously close to the time when the organs would no longer be viable. Conveying the urgency of the situation to the base commander, they were bundled into a helicopter and flown directly to downtown Seattle.

As the new day began, Will's young heart was transplanted into a 21-year-old man and both lungs into a 52-year-old. His liver and a kidney went to a 29-year-old man, his pancreas and another kidney to another 29-year-old, a father of two, and the corneas to two other patients.

Back in Anchorage, the team completed its work, carefully suturing Will's chest and abdomen, just as if he were still alive, applying dressings to the incisions and washing his body, returning it as much as possible to the state it was in prior to the donation.

Then Will was put gently into a shroud, having just saved the lives of four people it's hard to imagine he would ever have met.

Transplants Unite Jews and Muslims

The setting was unlikely: a hotel lobby in the Italian Alps five years ago, where a family of Muslims from Israel was sipping coffee with two Jewish Israeli families. They were talking quietly, as friends do, about the kind of personal experiences that transcend race, religion and politics.

What brought the families together was even more unlikely: one by one, five of their children had fallen so ill that only the organs of five other people, who had died suddenly, had saved their lives. They had met in the Schneider Children's Memorial Center near Tel Aviv, whose mission statement allows for no racial discrimination between patients and where the kidneys and livers were transplanted into the sickest children.

"We were one big family at the hospital," Judy, one of the Jewish mothers commented. Listening to the hushed conversation and watching the smiles of the children, as the snow fell steadily outside, the ethnic killings that could threaten any of them seemed very far away.

They were in Italy for the unlikeliest reason of all: a series of ski races for children who have received a new organ, 38 of them from 18 countries. At one time all had been desperately ill. Some had frightened their parents from the first moment they saw them: some were blue at birth, some yellow, some a frightening shade of green. Time and again their parents had to remind themselves: "We may not have this baby long."

Some of the children had spent almost half their lives in hospitals. At one time one of the 14-year-old boys was taking 40 different medications a day. Even at eight years old, Nicholas from Australia had already had a bone marrow transplant, cataract operations to stave off blindness, hips pinned because of degeneration of the joints, cancer of the abdomen and the loss of a kidney. Because of the resulting complications, he could not be sedated and for even relatively minor procedures needed a general anesthetic: more than a hundred of them in one 12-month period.

Others in the group had lived a perfectly normal life, until they had suddenly been felled by a virus that at first seemed no more serious than a common cold. In some cases the real problem went undetected for months. "We just thought he was a plump baby," one father said. Instead it was incipient liver failure.

Whatever their medical history, by the time they needed a transplant the end was in sight. Some could scarcely lift their heads from the pillow. Others were given only a day or two to live.

At that time, the idea that these children, whose ages ranged from 5 to 16, could play a competitive sport, let alone race down a 30-degree slope, 6,000 feet up in the mountains, would have seemed preposterous. Many had never been on skis before. Yet here they were competing in a giant slalom on a course that even many normal, healthy children would have found impossible.

The competition was started in 2001 by Liz Schick, a British-born mother of two, living in Switzerland, whose life had been saved by a liver transplant, and was organized by the World Transplant Games Federation, an affiliate of the International Olympic Committee. The federation was started in 1978 by a pioneer transplant surgeon, Dr. Maurice Slapak of Britain, who was struck by the fact that one of his patients, whom he had transplanted only a few months earlier, easily kept up with him when they were out jogging.

For Slapak, very fit and a former Cambridge University tennis and hockey player, it was a seminal moment. Since then, the federation has organized transplant games around the world every two years. "I wanted to show in the most memorable way that most organ transplants restore the recipients to full health," he says. "Most of these children can do anything normal kids do."

It is not always straightforward, however. After years of waiting, Judy's son, Michael, received a liver and a kidney. Within weeks both failed and his chances of finding two more donors plunged toward zero. Against all odds, he was saved a second time by two more bereaved families. Meanwhile, however, his father, Simcha, died at the age of 39, after waiting in vain for a pancreas and kidney, and Judy was left to cope alone.

Fifteen-year-old Anthony, another of the Jewish boys, has had three new kidneys. When the first gave out, his father George donated one of his. Crushingly, it failed too. "I'd been so sure I could help him," George said, the weary helplessness of those days still evident in his tone. But, after six agonizing years, the family of a Jewish man killed in a terrorist attack donated the kidney that was keeping Anthony alive and a liver that went to an Arab.

In one week of training these neophytes were transformed. At the top of a steep, icy, twisting slope one of the little figures would take a deep breath, break away from the group and head straight down the mountainside. Some attacked with everything they had, poles flailing, skis clattering dangerously around the sharp bends. Others snowplowed with infinite caution.

All fought to win — they wouldn't be alive if they weren't fighters — but everyone knew the competition was not about the fastest times but about a medical wonder and the human spirit that can transform tragedy into triumph. "Every day is a miracle for us," said Piero, a kidney recipient, as he watched the children compete. His eyes clouded with tears as he hugged his cherubic six-year-old daughter, Alessia, who, if things had gone differently, might never have been born.

Lung Recipient Runs Up Skyscraper

"I was sick all my life," says Steve Ferkau, manager of trading floor operations at the Chicago Stock Exchange. "As a child I was always coughing and getting serious infections. I had bronchitis, allergies and bouts of pneumonia. I was very thin, and as far back as I can remember I was always the smallest in the class. At 16, when I got my driver's license, I weighed 75 pounds."

On his 13th birthday, his problems were diagnosed as cystic fibrosis, the genetic disease that produces thick sticky mucus that clogs the lungs. Thirty thousand Americans suffer from it.

The treatment was a form of torture for everyone involved. Every day someone had to pound on his chest so he could cough up the gooey mess to clear his lungs. "Mom had no rhythm, so at 7 o'clock, nearly every morning for six years, Dad cupped his hands and thumped my chest until he left for work. At 10 o'clock at night he did another half hour."

In time Steve had learned to do most of the pounding himself and for years he estimates he too spent 40 to 60 minutes, twice a day, on it. At least once a year he spent 10 to 14 days in a hospital to clean out the system more thoroughly with a more intensive therapy regimen and I.V. antibiotics. "After these tune-ups, I'd feel much better. But only for a short while."

When he was 18, his left lung collapsed. It was repaired but collapsed again two years later. The experience was so disturbing that he made a vow to himself, "If this happens again, I won't get it fixed." It wasn't the pain he worried about, he says, as much as the fear that they might not be able to fix the next problem he encountered.

In those years, he faced an even bigger dilemma. "With my illness, I'd never felt worthy of a serious one-on-one relationship. It always seemed unfair to saddle someone with the problems I was likely to face." So when he met and fell in love with Laura Ikens, who also worked at the stock exchange, he knew they had to have a long talk before things went much further. "I may not be here in five years," he told her. "I'll be very, very lucky to make it to 10."

Laura understood. She knew she could become a young widow but decided to take whatever amount of time she could have with him. In March 1989, they were married. By this time his lungs were working at less than 50 percent of expected capacity. "But I still got around. I still enjoyed life. I could play golf and be reasonably active."

Then, in 1996, he suffered another collapse, this time in his right lung. Despite his vow, he went into the hospital again. "By then I'd learned that love trumps fear. I couldn't bear the thought of leaving Laura," he explains. "But after that operation, I never came back to where I had been. Before that, I used to walk the five blocks to work in about 15 minutes. It now took an hour. Every night, Laura came to meet me at work and walk home with me. It was no fun in a Chicago winter."

In May 1997, during a therapy treatment, a major blood vessel ruptured and blood poured into his lungs. He was whisked to the emergency room at Rush University Medical Center and again fixed up. But this time his doctor, who had looked after him for 28 years, told him, "It's time." Steve knew what he meant. They had discussed his possible need for a transplant over the years but had agreed that he wasn't ready. Now the new worry was whether they had waited too long.

Once you get on the waiting list, it will be the worst year of your life, the doctor told him. It was, Steve agrees, but neither of them imagined it would be almost three years.

By now, a physical therapist was coming to Steve's house seven days a week, twice a day, to pound on his chest. After work, Laura would do a session and, at night, Steve's sister would drive over to do another. "That went on for three straight years," he says.

All the time he was deteriorating. For the three years before his transplant, he was on oxygen 24 hours a day. Just to get up off the sofa, where he spent a lot of time, and walk to the bathroom left him crouched over the sink struggling to catch his breath. His coughs were bone-racking.

"Every night I sat in bed and said my prayers while I wound down. I'd pray that my future donor was enjoying life. And that I might hold out just a little bit longer to let them finish what they needed to finish. I knew that someone had to pass away for my life to be saved and that can never be an easy thought. But I prayed that, when that did happen, the family would have the strength to make the decision that would help me and keep me here with Laura a little longer."

He carried a pager at all times so that he could go into the hospital immediately if a set of lungs were offered. "At first, it's a nerve-wracking business waiting for the ring and knowing that every day it didn't go off you're a day nearer dying." After 20 months on the waiting list, it finally did ring and an excited voice said, "Come on in, Steve. We've got some lungs."

Laura packed up everything, making sure she hadn't forgotten any of the items on which his life depended. "I was too weak to help. I just sat there and tried not to think about what might go wrong. Laura called my family and hers and everybody converged on the hospital."

He was prepped for surgery and his optimism swamped the fear he felt. Then the nurse walked in and said, "I'm sorry, Steve. Those lungs didn't work out. I'm afraid you'll have to get dressed and go home."

It could have been worse, he says. "The transplant team warns you this might happen." Penny Pearson, who was Steve's transplant coordinator, confirms this is standard procedure. "We tell all patients from the start that they are unlikely to go home with new lungs the first time," she says. "They may be damaged or infected or perhaps just not a good match."

All the same, it's a potentially shattering experience and he was called in three times more on false alarms. "And every time I went in it was on my mind that there was a family out there who was devastated and who, despite all they were going through, was reaching out to help me." By now his lung capacity had deteriorated so much that death seemed just weeks away.

On April 7, 2000, 400 miles away, in Algona, Iowa, a beautiful 17-year-old girl, Kari Westberg, was in her warm and comfortable home but with a fierce spring blizzard blowing across the plains. She woke with a headache and stayed in bed but consoled herself with the thought of wearing her new dress at the prom that Saturday. But Tylenol didn't help and, in a frighteningly fast progression, she complained of dizziness, then began talking incoherently and had a seizure.

"We dialed 911 but the helicopter couldn't get through," says Lisa, her mother. "Her eyes were fixed and dilated. She was a total dead weight. My husband and I were numb with shock. The ambulance came and drove her to Mason City, about an hour and a half away, through the snowstorm. We followed on in our own car. Alyssa, her older sister, insisted on coming, too. We scarcely spoke on the way. It seemed as though we'd never get there."

The end came brutally and without preamble. A blood vessel in her brain had burst. She'd had massive bleeding. There was no brain activity. "They told us that she was probably born with a malformation but could have gone all her life without any problem from it."

As it was, there had been no hint. She was a powerful hitter on the school volleyball team, went running regularly, played French horn in the school band and had a job as a waitress in a pizza parlor in town. She was in the top 10 percent of her class and a member of the National Honor Society. "She truly enjoyed everything life had to offer," says Lisa. "She was as healthy as a horse!"

Now she appeared to be breathing only because a ventilator was forcing air into her lungs. When it stopped, so would the up and down movement of her chest. The surgeon's words were absolute in their finality. "You should be thinking about whether you want her to be an organ donor," he said.

As it happened, that was something none of them did have to think about. A month or so before, the subject of donating organs came up at the supper table, prompted perhaps by the fact that the wife of a teacher at the school had had a kidney transplant. Kari was emphatic. "Why wouldn't you give someone else a chance if you didn't need them anymore?" she asked.

Lisa remembers, too, that when the two girls were comparing drivers' licenses, Kari "was all over Alyssa" for not having signed to be a donor. "So we all knew what she wanted. She'd already made the decision for us." Her heart, kidneys, liver, pancreas and some veins were donated.

In a town of 6,000 people, 700 came to her funeral service. Many of them said what they would always remember most about her was her radiant smile.

The lungs were allocated to Steve Ferkau, whose own lungs were now so clogged that Penny, the coordinator, still doesn't know how he pulled air through them.

All through his ordeal those who knew him agree his optimism was remarkable. "He never complained, even on those four false alarms – he just thanked us for trying. It's a deflating time for us, too, and he saw that. He was always encouraging us, when with most patients we have to be reassuring them," says Penny.

Since his transplant, his spirits have been sky high. "As with most successful lung transplants he was pink immediately," she recalls. Three weeks after the operation, he walked a mile in 20 minutes, something that before the transplant could have taken hours. In ten weeks he was back at work.

In February 2003, in an event staged by the American Lung Association of Metropolitan Chicago, he raced up 94 floors of the Hancock Center – 1,632 steps -- in 33 minutes. He could have done it in less time but he couldn't resist stopping every time he met a volunteer in the stairwell to say how grateful he and other people with lung disease were for the work they were doing – and, he adds, he also wanted to tell them about Kari.

Only the thought that such a beautiful person died clouds his happiness. Like many recipients, he wrote to the donor family, anonymously at first. He struggled to find the words. Everything seemed trivial compared with their loss. But eventually, he put his feelings like this: "After 40 years of living with cystic fibrosis, I hope you can understand what you've done for me. You did not just save my life. You've given me a life I've never known. I've never, ever, been able to breathe this well."

It's been over seven years and he is still pinching himself to make sure it is all real. "Nowadays I open my eyes in the morning, stretch and take a breath – and I don't hear my chest gurgling! I still walk around in complete awe of how this feels. There is a double flight of stairs from the trading floor to my office that I hadn't climbed in 10 years. I didn't even go down them in the last five years before my transplant. Now, every chance I get, I bound up those stairs two steps at a time."

Does he feel guilty, as so many recipients do, at living, while Kari has gone? "I'd have to say yes. It seems wrong that she is not with her family and I am finally experiencing such an incredible life."

But, if anything could, Lisa's reassurances to him and the other recipients should have put those anxieties to rest. "We never want them to feel they owe us," Lisa says in her unaffected way. "Their happiness is gratification enough."

Kari's heart recipient, Sandy Halstead, then 50 and living just a few miles away in Cylinder, Iowa, came even closer to missing the Westbergs' gift. After two heart attacks, she was getting weaker and weaker throughout 1999. "I was out of breath even brushing my teeth," she says.

Even so, she was horrified to be told she needed a transplant. "We didn't know anything about it. We didn't know anyone who had had one." But just as she was getting used to the idea that it was the only way to stay alive, she developed blood clots in her lungs and became so ill her doctors removed her from the waiting list. She could not have withstood a transplant operation even if a heart had become available.

"That was even more frightening," she recalls. Later she was told she was within two days of death. She was saved only by aggressive medication and a nine-hour operation to attach a pump to her weakening heart. Her doctors put her back on the list the day before Kari died.

Sandy's husband, Roger, works at Snap-On Tools, as does Kari's father, Larry. In such a small area it was clear, when Sandy got her transplant, who the donor was. Seven years later she still cries when she talks about Kari. But, in all other respects, says she feels "wonderful." She, too, is grateful for the evident pleasure the Westbergs show in her recovery. The two couples meet from time to time and Lisa says it does her good to hear her daughter's heart beating so steadily. "It makes me think she's still plugging away."

After Kari died, Lisa went to only one more volleyball game. "It's all I could manage," she says. Even now the pain is still raw, covered up most of the time, but liable to open on even the simplest stimulus – a song on the radio, perhaps, or seeing one of her friends. Sometimes Larry sees a car like hers and before he can check it says to himself, "There's Kari."

As for Steve, he still struggles to find some ground where he can tell them how happy he is without reminding them of what they've lost. But what he wrote to them must come as near to that hallowed ground as any poet could find: "You've taught me there is pure goodness in the world."

Nurse Helps Recipients Find a New Way of Life

Asking the parents of a three-year-old girl, killed in a heart-rending accident, to donate her organs, was one of the hardest things Penny Pearson has ever had to do.

While working for the organ procurement organization based in Chicago, now called the Gift of Hope Organ and Tissue Donor Network, she had made many of these requests. "I would attempt to put a tight lid on my emotions and always tried to remember it wasn't my job to persuade families to say yes, but just to give them all the facts they needed to make an informed choice and do what felt right to them. That put the decision where it should be - on them."

However, even after these parents agreed to the donation, the lid wouldn't stay on in this case. During the donation process, she spent several hours talking to them. While she was in the operating room, she thought of the stories they had told her about their daughter's sense of humor and exuberant personality and the photos they had shown of her.

They had asked to see her one last time after the donation. When the operation was finished, Penny washed the child's hair and wrapped her in warm blankets so they wouldn't be shocked by how cold she was. "When I lifted her up from the operating room table to the gurney, I realized they must have held her this same way hundreds of times," she says.

"When I wheeled her into the visitation room, they still had the cuddly toy they'd brought with them. It was a tearful moment for everyone. But I think it gave them a little comfort."

This ability to identify with other people's feelings is also one of the key requirements for the work she has done since then on the other side of transplantation, taking care of a wide range of kidney, pancreas and lung recipients at the University of Chicago Medical Center.

"Patients don't know what to expect the first time we see them in the clinic after their transplant. Many of them are still stunned that they actually received an organ and then we throw an entirely new way of life at them. They are in some pain, walking slowly, usually with a family member helping them. For the first few months, they are acutely aware of what can go wrong. This is the time when the risk of rejection is greatest. They worry a lot about catching colds and getting sick.

"Their new lifestyle includes many new medications. On average, we add 10 or 12 different drugs to what they are already taking for other ailments, like high blood pressure. In the next few months we wean them off many of these and reduce the dosages of others, but the immunosuppressants are new and they have to learn to take them regularly and know what each one is for.

"Even with all the changes and responsibilities that go along with being a recipient, within a couple of weeks of their operation they are startled by what their new life has opened up. Some of the kidney patients have been on dialysis for ten years or more. So, for one thing, they've had a tightly controlled diet all that time – no milk or sodas, for example, and only very small portions of many other foods. Now, within reason, they can eat almost anything.

"For another, they are beginning to break free of restrictive habits. The diabetics are so used to checking their blood sugar levels three times a day that many of them can't stop after their pancreas transplant. They find it hard to believe it when we tell them those days are over. Best of all, they don't have to spend three to six hours a day, three days a week, tied to a dialysis machine.

"Soon they can run and play games, things some of them have hardly known. It's wonderful to see people, who were so pale and nervous when you first met them, now laughing and planning a skiing trip to Colorado. After ten years in transplantation, I'm still amazed that it works so well.

"Often the whole dynamic of their household alters, as they start to play a full part again. The transplant heals marriages and friendships. So the second chance is not just that the kidneys or lungs are working properly. It affects the whole of life.

"They aren't home free, of course. We keep close tabs on them, looking for any signs of rejection or infection or complications of any kind. For the rest of their lives we'll be working with their primary care physicians to make sure their numbers are where they should be.

"We have to keep after some of them. Teenagers are particularly prone to saying, 'I don't like taking all these meds. I've had no problems at all. I'm going to try without and I'll bet you anything it will be fine.' But, in general, recipients are very responsible. They haven't forgotten how miserable their life once was. And they say to themselves, 'I owe it to my donor.'

"Right from the beginning, when they are still recovering from a pretty hard surgery, they think a lot about their donors. They are often emotional talking about them. How soon can we write to them? Can you tell me anything more about them? It's impressive how much they think about what's been given to them.

"We encourage them to write to the donor families - anonymously until both sides are willing to give their names – but it's often very hard for them to find the words. They agonize over what's appropriate. Should they draw attention to how they were rescued from death to a family still aching from an equally sudden loss? How can they say thank you adequately for such a huge gift? To help them, we put together a book of letters that other recipients have written that are very moving. But I can only remember two people using it in the past year. However hard they struggle, they want to say it their own way.

"Anyone who doubts the value of transplantation should see people who are approaching the top of the list. With time closing in, they're terrified they aren't going to make it. Some show it by anger: 'I've been on the list for three years, why am I still waiting?' Or worrying about everything: 'I can't breathe,' 'This is taking too long,' 'Did you forget about me?' The families of some patients call me almost every week to ask things like: 'Where is she on the list? Do you know when it will be? Can you guess?' They know I can't. They just need reassurance.

"Their fears are understandable. It can go either way. We had a 32-year-old cystic fibrosis patient who had been on the list three years and became so sick they flew him in from an out-of-state hospital in hopes that lungs would come up in time. He was blue and couldn't speak more than two words in a row. While he was in the ICU, steadily getting worse, I got multiple calls from organ procurement groups offering lungs. However, all of them turned out to be unsuitable.

"Then an offer came in for a beautiful pair of lungs that matched his blood type and size. I called the pulmonologist to make sure he would accept them and the surgeon to be sure that he was available.

"Then I called the ICU. The man had died three hours earlier. All I could think was, 'If only we could have had a few more hours.'"

Death – and Hope – in the Middle East

When the doorbell rang in John Boria's house in Broken Arrow, Oklahoma, on August 31, 2004, and he saw three National Guard Air Force colonels standing there, his first thought was that they had come to the wrong address. The second, a moment later, came with sickening force: "Has something happened to my son?" he asked.

Yes, they told him, something has happened. The Boria's elder son, Capt. John Javier 'Javy' Boria, a 29-year-old Air Force pilot, had been injured in an off-duty accident in an all-terrain vehicle he was driving in Qatar, where he was based.

They didn't know how serious the accident was but he was unconscious and they were ready to help John and his wife, Wanda, travel there as soon as a military plane was available. The alternative was a commercial flight.   But with flights overbooked into Qatar, a strategic planning center for the entire Middle East, that option seemed too risky.

The wait turned out to be two agonizing days for the Borias, with hope and fear alternating in rapid succession. They talked to members of their family, seeking support, turning over and over in their minds the little they knew and praying fervently. They remembered how proud they had been when Javy was accepted at the Air Force Academy and later how fearful they were when he flew missions over Afghanistan and Iraq.

"I envisioned some sort of coma and I just wanted to be with him, to talk to him, to bring him back," says John. He managed to telephone the hospital and had them place the phone close to Javy's ear while he and Wanda talked to him.

Their words were a jumble of choked emotions. "I love you very much. We're all praying for you," John remembers saying. "Hang in there, son. We'll be with you soon." But his heart was heavy and he could hear in the background the beep of the machines that were monitoring his son's fragile hold on life. Wanda, a nurse, suspected that things were even worse than John imagined.

The plane ride, though exhausting, gave some relief with its promise of an end to the gnawing uncertainty. When they entered the Hamad Medical Center in Doha, Wanda was encouraged by meeting experienced doctors from around the world and seeing state-of-the-art medical equipment.

But their hopes were short-lived. The chief doctor assigned to the case didn't waste time on a preamble. "I'm sorry to tell you that your son is brain dead," she said. "There's nothing we can do."

"It hit me like a rock," says John. "All those hopes that had been building up suddenly collapsed. We had been hoping for a miracle. I'd even brought a camera with me to take some pictures of him hooked up to all those machines so, when he was healed, we could use them as a testimony. Now that was all over."

The doctors had one more thing to tell them. They had discovered that on his driver's license Javy had indicated his willingness to be an organ donor. "But we won't do anything without your approval," they said.

For the Borias it seemed simple. "We said, 'Of course.' Those were his wishes." But they added a condition. "Our other son, Joey, is on his way here. We have to wait until he arrives." It was now six days after the accident and the hospital was worried that the organs might seriously deteriorate. Despite their misgivings, however, they agreed to wait.

Joey had come on the first commercial flight directly from bible school in Florida and, like his parents when they first arrived, was full of hope. He was devastated to learn they were waiting only for him to see Javy before the ventilator was turned off.

"It seemed so cruel to tell him that we didn't even have much time left," John says. "We went straight to the hospital and let him stay with his brother for as long as we could. But after only an hour we had to tell him, 'You must say your goodbyes now or those organs won't be of any use to anyone.'"

The word flashed around the hospital that the American family was donating the organs and that they were going to Arab families. In a region where donation is a rarity, the lives of four Arabs were saved and the sight of two others restored. One of the recipient families was so overcome with emotion that they offered the Borias money but were asked politely to give it to a charity instead.

Others not directly affected were moved, too. The mother of a boy who had been in a coma for months broke with custom to take off her veil and embrace Wanda. "Allah has been good to you," she said. "My son is alive but he is not here. Your son will give life to others."

To John the crossing of boundaries seems perfectly natural. "My family and Wanda's came from Puerto Rico and Javy was proud of his heritage. But the color of someone's skin never mattered to him. His donation was color blind, too."

Little Alexa, Sick from Birth

Little Alexa Kersting was plagued with problems from the start. "When she was born, she didn't pink up as she should have done," says her mother, Monica. Tests quickly established that one lung was collapsed. Instead of going home, she was put in the neonatal intensive care unit at Merit Care Hospital in Fargo, North Dakota.

But worrying as this was, she was not her parents' only cause for anxiety. At the time of her birth, her three-year-old brother, Dane, had been in a drug-induced coma for two weeks in the pediatric ICU of the same hospital, in an attempt to cure a series of seizures caused by Angelman syndrome, a neurological disease characterized by severe learning difficulties and an excitable personality. For the next 10 days, Monica and her husband, Loren, scarcely left the hospital.

By then both children were well enough to go home, though both needed careful watching. A respiratory virus, which developed into pneumonia, put Alexa back in the hospital. With that behind her, for a few years she acted like a normal toddler, running, jumping and playing around the house.

In time, however, it became obvious that she wasn't normal. She was often short of breath and prone to coughing after a burst of activity. Many tests followed and she was diagnosed with interstitial lung disease, a catch-all term for a wide range of chronic lung disorders. She began using oxygen for a part of every day.

"Knowing so little made it even more worrying," Monica says. Many tests, many journeys to hospitals as far away as Denver and Minneapolis and many treatments followed. But the illness was steadily progressing.

In time she was not only not gaining weight but losing it. She found it more and more difficult to breathe. She lacked the energy to eat. By the time she was 12, her condition was serious enough for a feeding tube to be inserted in her stomach. "She told no one about that, no one. She was too embarrassed," Monica says.

Meanwhile, Dane, suffering from his own affliction, developed such a severe case of scoliosis that he needed major surgery to straighten his spine. "It was a stressful time," Monica says. But it was about to get worse.

On a visit to the University of Minnesota Medical Center, Fairview, Alexa was found to have pulmonary hypertension, secondary to her lung disease. Now her only hope was a transplant. The news came like a thunderclap. "Alexa was a very intelligent girl. She was always aware of what was going on," Loren says. "She would never allow us to talk to the doctors without being there herself. So when she heard the diagnosis at the same time we did, she could see that everything was at a new level of seriousness."

Alexa's doctors registered her on the transplant list in December 2003. "Everything was so hard for her, we began to wonder if she would ever make it," Monica says. "Just getting out of bed tired her out. I remember how frightened I was when she said to me, 'I just don't know how long I can go on doing this.'"

In May and June she was back in the hospital. "The doctors told us later that if she'd had a setback there, they probably couldn't have saved her," Loren says. But even then she was still an eager teenager. In the hospital her most pressing concern was that 250 miles away in Mandan a cousin was about to get married, an event she had been looking forward to for a year. "Mom, Dad, we've got to go to the wedding," she pleaded. With the hospital's permission, she was allowed out, with 12 tanks of oxygen stowed in the family car.

That visit was part of a pattern. Throughout the years, the Kerstings had striven to maintain as normal a routine as possible for the children. "She wanted so much to be like other kids that even when she was on the transplant list she loved to go to the lake where we have a cabin and take out the jet ski. So we fitted one up with a place for her oxygen equipment and that summer she zoomed around pulling her friends," Loren says.

"I also taught her to drive a car. In North Dakota kids can get a driving permit when they are 14. One day we saw a red convertible Mustang for sale on a parking lot. I bought it for her so that she would have it when she was 16 and could drive alone." His voice breaks as he pictures it.

He remembers equally vividly one night in July how animated she was at a family party, laughing and talking with friends and cousins. The next morning, however, her breathing was suddenly much worse. "Then she just fell apart," Monica adds. They called 911, the police and an ambulance came immediately; but by then Alexa, aged 14, was dead, one of the 18 people on the waiting list who died that day because the organ that could save them was not donated.

Although they have to fight the tears, Monica and Loren now speak at organ donation meetings whenever they can, teaching people how easy it is to sign up to be an organ donor. "We want to do whatever we can to make sure other people don't go through what we're going through," they say.

Blind for 48 Years, He Can See Again

On the day after Christmas 1944, in a corner of what became one of the most fiercely fought battles of World War II, a German mine blew up in Sergeant Harold Urick's face. It left him totally blind and he stayed that way for 48 years.

Harold's unit, the 303rd Engineers, had just crossed the redoubtable German defensive barrier, the Siegfried Line, when they were ordered to dig up and defuse mines.

He remembers every detail. "It was a bitterly cold day and the ground was frozen hard. There was a man on each side of me as we moved forward. I saw the mine – it was one of the small ones they used, just about a quarter pound -- and began digging it up very carefully with my bayonet. Suddenly I slipped on the icy ground. There was an explosion and everything went dark. I put my hands on my face. 'My God, I thought, what am I going to do now?'

"Most of all in those early days, I worried about Jean. I was 21 and we'd been married just over a year. I thought of it over and over. Instead of the life we'd dreamed of when the war was over, I was going to be a burden to her all her life."

He was flown to a military hospital in Valley Forge and then back home to Cleveland. One eye was so badly damaged that it to be taken out and a prosthetic one put in its place. With the other he could see just a patch of light.

He spent two years in a therapy school and then, with the dogged courage that has defined his life, started a physical therapy business of his own. "But people weren't as affluent then and it didn't take," he says. He worked for several years at the Cleveland Clinic and then for another 15 at a snack bar managed by the Cleveland Sight Center.

In the meantime, he and Jean had five children and seven grandchildren, none of whom he had ever seen. The family was central to his life. He went to almost every high school and college football game his son, Jeff, played in. "My wife would tell me what was going on. I just wanted to be there."

But his sight didn't improve. "I went to three or four ophthalmologists over the years but all of them said they couldn't do anything for me. Then one day in 1992 I was listening to a television program and I heard a doctor talking about transplanting corneas. I didn't know what to think but I went back to the eye doctors. They weren't encouraging until one of them said, 'I know a doctor who does these. I think you should go to him.'

"That's how I met Dr. Philip Shands at Kaiser Permanente. 'Yes,' he told me, 'I do these. Do you want to try?' 'You bet,' I said. 'What do I have to lose?'"

Shands had then been in practice for only a year or two and was unsure himself about how much he could help. "The prosthetic eye we could do nothing about, of course. But when I examined the other one, I could see a small bit of the iris which, when we shone a light on it, constricted a little. Then, using ultrasound and other tests, it appeared as though the retina and other structures inside the eye were intact."

With this encouragement, Harold was put on the waiting list and told it would probably take three or four months before they had a cornea for him. "You might think I'd be on pins and needles all that time but I wasn't. Most of the time I didn't think about it, probably because he exuded so much confidence," he recalls.

Just before Thanksgiving, he was called in and, with great care, Shands removed the badly damaged cornea and other scarred tissue, implanted an artificial lens to focus the light and sewed in the donated cornea. In about an hour it was all over, Harold remembers. "'Are you done?' I asked him. 'Yep,' he said 'but you'll have to wait until tomorrow morning when we remove the bandages.'

"The next day, when he began to take them off, I was lying face down on the bed and the first thing I saw were his shoes – the first things I'd seen in 48 years – then his pants. I looked up and saw he was wearing glasses. It was still a bit fuzzy, but they'd warned me it would take a while.

"Then I looked down the bed and there was Jean, looking as pretty as she did when I first met her. Then I looked at Yvonne, my oldest daughter. It was the first time I'd ever seen her face. And she was beautiful, too."

He had some shocks too, such as how big airplanes had become and how fast cars went. In a few months his sight had improved so that he could pass the driver's test and read just about anything he wanted. "Since then we've only had to fine-tune the prescriptions for his glasses, just like any normal aging person," Shands says. "With them on he has 20/25 vision. Like all corneal recipients, he takes small amounts of immunosuppressants but has never had a period of rejection."

The other patients Shands treats have much less dramatic stories. "This was a once-in-a-career case," he says. "But vision is the faculty people fear losing most and, with success rates of over 90 percent for those who are legally blind, cornea transplants reopen a world they thought they had lost forever."

All his life Harold has treasured the little things. Now it's being able to walk through a restaurant to find a table or waving at friends across the street. He can still see with only one eye but goes to baseball games regularly and doesn't need a running commentary. And at 86, he still bowls and plays golf.

"But best of all is being able to see the whole family," he says. "That was the hardest thing all those years. Now I have everything I want."

Nurse Still Shocked by How Sick Some Children Are

"I wanted to be a nurse when I was five years old. When I was 12, and one of my sisters went into a hospital, I was certain I was going to be a pediatric nurse. At nursing school, I concentrated on children's diseases. But none of that prepared me for how sick children really get."

Emily Jackson, now 27, has been a nurse at the UCLA Medical Center's pediatric intensive care unit and sedation room for five years and what she sees still shocks her. "We get babies in ventilators who can't be touched because their hearts can't handle it. They don't have the oxygen supply or vascular structure to tolerate anything other than simply being kept alive. We have to heavily sedate, or even paralyze, them or they couldn't live at all.

"In nursing school you learn about alcoholics who kill their livers but hardly anyone talks about the babies who are born with bad livers and bleed everywhere: they throw up blood, their diapers are bloody, they can bleed into their heads and die in a matter of seconds."

She treats children with kidneys that never develop and have to be put on dialysis from birth. Some with liver disease are so jaundiced their eyes are a glowing yellow. The 20-bed unit is always close to being full of critically ill patients ranging from brand-new babies to 21-year-olds.

"Most of them are candidates for an organ transplant and for them there's no other choice." Emily says. "But when we tell the parents that, we never know how they are going to react. Some are frightened, some refuse to believe it, some simply won't listen. But for most it's a relief that there's a way out of the suffering and, for some, the first hope they've had since the child was born.

"We get many very young parents and, as we know, it's hard for a child to bring up a child. But to bring up a sick child is a hundred times harder. They don't know what to think or how they are going to manage.

"Children are very resilient, however. If they can get a new organ, they usually can be fixed. I'd guess about 80 percent of the children who come to the ICU get to go home. But it's a waiting game and, with donated organs from babies so scarce, many of the smallest ones don't make it," she says.

"I've been to a lot of funerals. It's always very hard. I fall in love with almost every child I take care of so, although it's the parents who ask you to come, you go for yourself. When children have spent practically their whole life in hospital, it's the nurses who know them best."

Emily remembers one baby girl who was bleeding from multiple incisions from previous surgeries, was on a breathing machine and on multiple blood products to strengthen her liver and blood factors to help with clotting. "Her liver enzymes were through the roof. They were at toxic levels. She was so yellow she looked liked a yam. When he saw her, the surgeon said flatly, 'I can't transplant this baby until she is stronger. As she is now, she won't survive the surgery.' None of us expected her to live.

"But she was a fighter, and every day she got a little better. Eventually she sat up and we tailed off the medicines until she was healthy enough for a transplant. There were complications and for 24 hours it was touch and go. But now she's four years old and, unless you knew, you couldn't tell she'd ever been that close to death."

The work can be emotionally draining. "But when these children come back to see us, dressed in their best clothes, laughing and full of energy, it's the happiest feeling I know," she says. "I can't imagine doing anything else."

Life Out of Death on the Long Island Railroad

Soon after 7 o'clock on a bitterly cold night in December 1993, Jack Locicero, a retired public school teacher, was watching "Jeopardy" at home in Hawthorne, New Jersey, when the program was interrupted by a report of a shooting on a crowded commuter train in the New York area. An angry man with a semi-automatic pistol had opened fire, hitting 25 passengers, several of whom were in critical condition.

It crossed Jack's mind to wonder if his 27-year-old daughter Amy, who commuted between Long Island and Manhattan, might possibly have been involved. But he put the thought aside, thinking the shooting was on the New York subway.

But, as reports kept coming in, he heard it was the Long Island Railroad and the 5:33 p.m. from Pennsylvania Station, a train she might well have caught. Nervous, but still dismissing the fears as fanciful, he phoned her apartment and was told by her roommate, Peg, that Amy, who should by then have been home, was still out.

By now Jack couldn't get the fears out of his mind. Twenty minutes later Peg phoned to say Amy was one of the victims and was already in Winthrop University Hospital in Mineola. Jack's wife, Arlene, who had heard nothing about the shooting, came home at 9:25 p.m. from graduate school to be confronted by the news that her daughter was in the emergency room.

The two of them got into the car and drove the 40 miles to the hospital, Arlene resting her face from time to time on the cold window. An evangelical Christian who, like Jack, has been a member of the Hawthorne Gospel Church since before Amy was born, she now sought comfort by repeating to herself passages from the Bible. One sentence that came repeatedly to her mind was from Psalm 46. "Be still and know that I am God."

At the hospital, the medical teams were engulfed by the casualties but, for a second, the first sight of their daughter was reassuring. "There was color in her cheeks, her hair was tidy and she seemed to be breathing steadily," Arlene remembers. "But immediately afterward, I realized the ventilator was breathing for her." Looking closer, she froze at the sight of encrusted blood on Amy's fingers and feet.

Her parents learned that when she was brought into the hospital she had been in cardiac arrest and her brain had been deprived of blood for 35 minutes. The emergency room staff had jump-started her heart to keep her body functioning.

Arlene stayed at the hospital with Peg, who had come, too, while Jack got back into the car to drive to Pennsylvania, where their other daughter, Carrie, then 21, was at Gettysburg College. It didn't occur to him to telephone. "I wanted to be there when she heard the news," he explains.

He drove, alone with his thoughts, arriving at six in the morning. He sat in the car outside the dormitory until he saw a light go on.

Waking Carrie, he explained what had happened and the two of them drove another four hours back to the hospital, listening to updates about the shooting on the car radio as they went.

When they got there, Amy's condition was unchanged. "She looked so healthy that I found myself saying to her, 'Come on, Amy, come on, you can do it,'" Arlene says. Occasionally her eyelids would flutter and they would all feel a thrilling surge of hope. But the nurses told them it was an involuntary spasm and, as quickly as their hopes had been raised, they withered again. At one time, Arlene and Carrie sang to her some of the songs they knew from bible school. But, despite everything, on the fifth day all brain activity ceased.

At one point during the long vigil Peg asked quietly, "If this doesn't work out, have you thought about organ donation?" The idea was not a new one to the Locicero family because of a tragedy that Amy had suffered only a year earlier. After just three months of marriage, her 26-year-old husband, Gary, had died of pancreatic cancer. At that time they had discussed whether a transplant might save him, though in the end that proved not to be possible.

Now perhaps Amy could help someone else. As Jack puts it, "We knew very little about it but if we had been willing to receive a transplant from someone for Gary, shouldn't we be willing to give one, too?"

The family wanted one last verification that Amy was gone, however, and asked to be present when the ventilator was turned off. The doctors agreed. As they watched, it was clear that Amy couldn't breathe alone. In Arlene's words, "The hardest thing to do was to accept that she couldn't live. The decision to donate wasn't difficult at all. You come to the point where you realize it's the right thing to do and then we were able to let go."

Since then they have become ambassadors for organ and tissue donation and founding members of Transplant Speakers International, speaking at health fairs, schools and organ procurement groups and wherever else they see an opportunity to tell their story.

A year later, Amy's killer, Colin Ferguson, who had been overpowered by some of the passengers, was convicted and sentenced to six consecutive terms of life imprisonment. Asked how she feels about him now, Arlene says "He's where he ought to be, but we pray for his soul." She has written to him in that spirit but has had no reply and her last letter was returned with a 'delivery refused' stamp on it.

Three of Amy's four recipients have died, one of them a 55-year-old woman from the New York area, who suffered a respiratory infection only two months after the liver transplant. Another was Theresa Caravella of Islip, New York, who received the heart and, at the time of the transplant, had barely the strength to get out of bed. She lived 13 more years and every Mother's Day sent a bouquet with a card that said simply "From Amy's Heart." The third was 40-year-old Jerry Bradley, a carpenter from Glen Falls, New York, who received a kidney but died in 1996. The other kidney recipient, however, Betty Janko of Dallas, still keeps in touch with the Lociceros.

All three deaths hurt them, particularly Jerry's, who had become a close friend. But they never experienced the trauma some observers worry about. "We weren't losing Amy again. We were losing Jerry," says Jack. Both are emphatic that they did not feel their gift had been wasted in any way because of these deaths. "Transplantation isn't a perfect science," Arlene observes.

Although there is no sense of closure, the donations have eased the pain. "It's not like putting a bandage on a wound, which then heals," says Arlene. "But there is a sense of satisfaction that we were able to help."

She also has memories for solace. One is of Amy at six years old, on a swing in the yard, singing a favorite song: "I'm Bound for the Promised Land."

Dynamic Child Needed New Heart

Lacey Wood, born in May 1989 in Placerville, California, was a perfectly healthy baby for the first 10 months of her life. So when, one Saturday morning in the spring of 1990, she had a cold and seemed to be having difficulty breathing, her mother, Colleen, was concerned but not unduly worried. She took Lacey to the family doctor who, after a few routine tests, delivered a bombshell. "Meet me in the emergency room," he said. "I'm canceling all my other appointments for the day."

Shortly afterward, at the local hospital, a doctor looked up from reading the X-rays they had taken and said to Colleen, "We have a problem." "What's up?" she remembers saying, still unable to believe that her energetic child could be seriously ill. It was the last flippant remark she made for many months.

"Your child is in heart failure," the doctor told her. "We have to get her to the intensive care unit in Davis right away." As she and her husband, Grayson, scrambled into the ambulance, a nurse told the driver. "You've got to hurry. We're not sure she's going to make it to the hospital." The words made Colleen's blood run cold.

At the University of California Davis Medical Center, she could scarcely find the will to let Lacey go to be tested. After a wait that seemed interminable, a nurse came out to say, "Your baby is on life support." The news took her to a new low level.

She remembers more time passing, though most of it in a blur, until one of the doctors added more to worry about. "He told us they didn't know if she would come out of it and, if she did, how much heart function she would have." She and her husband were beside themselves with anxiety.

Another shock awaited them when they were allowed into the unit. "Lacey looked so tiny and there were tubes coming out of her everywhere," Colleen says. For a family with no history of heart disease and almost no experience of serious illness, it was a new world.

For three weeks Colleen sat in a rocking chair in Lacey's room. She didn't read or knit or talk on the telephone. She tidied the room and helped the nurses with routine tasks but mostly she spent hours staring at the heart monitor.

At last things took a turn for the better. The hospital took Lacey off life support and let her go home, but with a greater variety of medications than Colleen had ever thought possible and strict instructions to keep her from being too active. "The doctors said they still didn't know how strong her heart was. We would just have to wait and see."

Waiting and seeing was nerve-wracking, with constant worry about even the slightest change, until one day at the hospital a doctor said to them, "Lacey might be a candidate for a transplant." A few weeks before, that would have sounded terrifying. Now they grasped at it. "Do you mean there's a chance she can live?" they asked.

Lacey was evaluated by the transplant team at Stanford Hospital & Clinics. After determining she was a good candidate for a heart transplant, they added her to the list. But hearts for children, they quickly found out, were always very scarce. From time to time she would have a setback and they would have to go back into the intensive care unit at UC Davis.

"I heard children dying. It was horrible," Colleen says. "You'd always know. The pace would suddenly quicken, monitors would sound alarms, doctors and nurses would hurry into one of the rooms, their voices becoming more urgent. You could tell they were doing everything they could, but then you'd hear the parents sobbing, sometimes wailing, and the nurses consoling them. Then later just a dreadful emptiness about that room."

Disturbingly, several of the other children in the unit were potential organ donors. Colleen tried not to get too close to their families. "It's frightening to think that your child might be saved because one of those families might lose their own baby." Somehow she felt sure that if a heart came it would be from that small group of people.

She decided it would be better if she lived at Stanford, where the transplant would be done. The family carried a pager wherever they went. To their surprise and joy, within just a few days they had the news they were waiting for: Lacey had been matched with a heart that was on its way from Utah. They were scarcely able to believe it.

Then, a few hours later, a second message came. During the flight the heart had tested positive for hepatitis. They were devastated. "All the hopes that we had built up just crashed," Colleen says.

Four days later, in the middle of the night, the telephone rang. Another heart had been donated and allocated to Lacey. It was from

UC Davis. Consumed by conflicting emotions, they waited again. This time the heart was in perfect condition.

Later they found out that it had belonged to a 22-month-old boy who had slipped away from his mother and fallen through the railings of a balcony, three stories high.

For Lacey, life was transformed. Almost overnight she became healthy, happy and confident. When she was five, the children in her kindergarten class were asked to describe themselves by a word starting with the same letter as their own name. She chose lucky and has been Lucky Lacey to everyone ever since.

She has played basketball and volleyball for her high school, gone snowboarding in the nearby Sierra Nevada Mountains, ridden dirt bikes with fierce determination and played drums in the school band. "She'll try anything," Colleen says.

The Woods have written several times to the family of the donor but so far have had no reply. "I really would like them to see how their son's life goes on in me," Lacey says. "I'm so thankful to them that I can't find the words to say it."

Then three years ago, her life began to change again. She started to feel she was losing some of her dynamic energy. She felt more tired than she should have been, less interested in new challenges. Tests revealed blood clots in her arms and legs and she spent three months in the hospital. It became apparent that now her kidneys, which had never given her any trouble before, were failing, probably because of the high doses of immunosuppressants that were common 15 years ago.

Colleen and Grayson hoped they would be a match but another voice made itself heard. Lacey's brother, Tyson, two years older than she, was determined to help. "I want her to get better," he kept saying. To his frustration, he discovered that he could not be a living kidney donor until he was 18.

But when that day came, without hesitation, he went through with the donation. Tests showed his kidneys matched hers by every measure. "Now I know I'm Lucky Lacey," she says, "having a brother who would do that for me and being a perfect match, too."

Daughter's Decision Saves Father's Life

When the telephone in Chet Szuber's home in Berkley, Michigan, rang at 4:45 one Tuesday morning in 1994, he said to his wife, Jeanne, "It's got to be a wrong number. Don't answer it."

His indifference is understandable. At the time, he had been on the waiting list for a new heart for four years. He'd suffered two major heart attacks and three bypass operations. At 42, he was forced to retire. By now, at 58, he could hardly walk up a flight of stairs. Bending over to wash his face had him panting for breath. By noon every day he was done in.

But for Jeanne, the ringing was an alarm bell. She went into the kitchen to answer it – and stayed there. Making the effort, Chet got out of bed to find out what had happened. Even then, he had no inkling of what was to come. Jeanne looked up, her face white with shock. "Patti's been in a bad accident," was all she could say, handing him the phone, and walked into the living room.

In disbelief, Chet heard a voice at the University of Knoxville Hospital say, "Your daughter's death appears to be but moments away." He and Jeanne stayed just where they were, he on a kitchen chair, she in the living room, too stunned to move.

After a while, they saw they had a lot to do. They woke their other daughter, Janette, and then one by one phoned their four sons, all of whom lived nearby. Soon the entire family had come together, trying to absorb the news that the baby of the family, 22 years old and just starting her career as a nurse, who had gone to the Great Smokey Mountains on a camping trip, might be the first of them to die.

While they talked, Chet remembered that four years earlier Patti had told him she had just signed her donor card. "That's nice," he told her and forgot about it. Now he couldn't get it out of his mind. That was something they could do for her, he thought. He telephoned the doctor he had spoken to earlier. "Please do everything humanly possible to save that child," he managed to say, "but if things don't work out, I want you to know it was her desire to be an organ donor."

Two of the boys caught the next flight from Detroit and Chet and Jeanne followed the next day. "I was afraid he wouldn't survive the journey," she says.

At the hospital they learned that on a winding mountain road, the car Patti was in had hit a granite cliff by the side of the road and rolled over. She had been thrown on to the road and her brain was severely damaged. The ventilator was keeping her breathing regular. Rick, the youngest brother, had sat up with her all night, holding her hand and touching her brow but she was totally unresponsive.

More family members and Patti's friends kept arriving, until in time 17 of them were in the hospital. On Saturday, she was given the last rites of the Catholic Church. On Sunday, death was pronounced. Chet signed the consent forms to donate Patti's organs although, he says, it was "the hardest signature I've ever given." In doing so, her heart, kidneys, liver and corneas were donated.

As they walked out, Chet remembers Susie, a transplant coordinator from Tennessee Donor Services, running up to him and saying, "I know you've been waiting for a heart for four years. There's something called 'directed donation,' which allows donors to designate recipients for their organs. You can have Patti's heart."

He was shocked at the idea. "How could I do that, with every heart beat reminding me of her?" he thought. He quickly said no, to Susie's obvious disappointment, and walked slowly down the long corridor to the elevator.

It turned out to be a fateful walk. "I don't want to be corny," he says now, "but I felt that at that moment Patti was pleading with me to accept her gift. It's hard to remember all the things that went through my mind. Is this right, I wondered. Is it selfish? What will the family say?" He went back to the room to try to see his way through the maze.

The idea worried Jeanne. "We'd always been told that because he's such a big man he needed the heart of another big person. He's 6 feet tall and, even when he was so sick, he weighed close to 180 pounds. Patti was only 5 feet,1 inch. I didn't want to lose him, too."

But she got all the children together and Chet said it was up to them to decide. "It has to be unanimous. If anyone objects, I won't do it." There was a pause. Then somebody said, "You've got to do it, Dad." That, it turned out, was what everyone thought.

He returned to Michigan and Dr. Jeffrey Altshuler from the William Beaumont Hospital in Royal Oak flew to Tennessee. "Please be gentle," Chet said to him. At 4 a.m. on Monday, he removed Patti's strong young heart. At 6 a.m., Chet was taken into the operating room. "At 9:10 a.m.," he says, his voice choking, "her heart beat for the first time inside me."

From the moment he woke from surgery, he couldn't believe how well he felt and how clear his mind was. "Before, with the heart not pumping enough oxygen to the brain, my retention was shocking. I'd read a paragraph and then couldn't remember what was in it.

"Less than three months later, I was hunting deer in northern Michigan, something I'd had to quit years before because I couldn't even walk to the blind. In just over a year, I was hunting caribou in northern Quebec, where there are only rocks and water and stunted trees -- no place for a sick person.

"I swing at a golf ball as hard as I ever did and I made a promise to myself that I'd never get angry at a bad shot. I mostly kept that promise because I never forget that the Grim Reaper has been trying to catch me for 35 years."

Although he was a heating and cooling salesman for much of his life, he studied farming while he was sick and bravely started a 400-acre Christmas tree farm that is now a thriving business. He has traveled the world on speaking engagements, proving by his presence alone the power of transplantation. "In all those years I haven't had an ounce of rejection. It feels as though this heart can go on forever," he says.

"Best of all, I can be with my grandkids. Until then I wasn't a very good grandfather. It wasn't that I didn't love them. I just couldn't interact with them, couldn't carry or keep up with them. Now there are 12 of them, ranging from two years to18, and I can do anything they want me to."

He is always conscious of Patti being a part of him and, after 13 years, tears often come to his eyes when he tries to say something about her. "But I'm sure this is what she would have wanted," he adds. And, though it gives him chills when he thinks about it, he remembers that after the transplant several of her friends came to see him to say she had told them how sick he was and that she wished she could help him get better. "She's doing more for me than she could ever have imagined," he says.

The Day They Shot Shafeeq

For four long months Larry Montgomery, a white dentist, 39 years old and a father of three young boys, lay in the intensive care unit at Philadelphia's Temple University Hospital with a wasting heart. The same disease had killed his father and 35-year-old brother.

By now his own heart was beyond repair. Only a new healthy one could save him and he worried that the odds against one becoming available in time were formidably high.

"It was very frightening," he recalls. "Patients who came into the hospital needing a heart transplant, like me, died while they waited." One man admitted one day to the next bed died overnight. "I only shook his hand once and, when I came back in the room, he was gone."

A few miles away in South Philadelphia, an exuberant 15-year-old African-American boy, Shafeeq Murrell, was bounding out of his front door, headed to a pick-up basketball game. It was the wrong day. Without warning, Shafeeq stepped into a cross-fire of rival drug gangs and was shot in the head.

Gail, his mother, just home from using a gift certificate for her son at Eddie Bauer's, was startled to hear a neighbor pounding on her door and then, almost uncomprehendingly, hearing her cry over and over. "They've shot Shafeeq, come quick, they've shot Shafeeq."

Shaking with fear, Gail ran into the street. "It's only a block and a half but it seemed like ten," she says. "When I got there he was lying on the ground. Everyone stepped back – they all stepped back – it felt as though I was alone with him. I knelt down next to him. 'You're going to be okay, Shafeeq,' I kept telling him. 'You're going to be okay.'"

But at the hospital he wasn't okay. "'We're trying to get the swelling in his brain down,' the doctors told us. But they didn't get the swelling down. They never got the swelling down."

Gail still struggles to describe how a boy as kind and considerate as Shafeeq, with so much to give, should have ended his journey there. "At the funeral, there was an elderly couple we didn't know," she says. "They came over to us to tell how one day Shafeeq had seen the lady struggling to carry her groceries home. After that, he went to the store for them once a week. He never said anything to us about it – and he never took anything for it."

He left the same impression on the people at the city housing agency, where he had been a summer intern, but was so well liked that, exceptionally, he was put on the permanent payroll. A woman, who worked with him, recalls how he walked her to the subway most nights because he was concerned about her safety.

Now Shafeeq's parents had another test to face. Stacey, their daughter, was a nurse and had known before they did that he was unlikely to pull through. When the doctors confirmed that he was dead, she braced herself to ask a question even many of the most experienced organ donation professionals find difficult.

But it had to be done now or not at all, she thought. Summoning up her courage, she asked them outright. "Shall we donate his organs? It could save other families from what we're going through." Shocking though the request can be to people in the depths of grief, their answer was clear. "Of course."

"I'd read about organ donation, seen it on television, but I'd never given it a second's thought," Gail says now. "But in my heart I knew it was the right thing to do."

Over at Temple, Larry was thinking about his coming birthday, aware that more likely than not it would be his last, when he suddenly heard these words: "We think we have a heart for you." His mind filled with a jumble of emotions but among them one somber thought was always there: "Someone had to die to give me this chance."

All he knew about that someone was that it was a 15-year-old, though later he became convinced that it was the 15-year-old from Wharton Street whose death, the day he got his new heart, was reported in the newspaper. The transplant was fraught with more danger than most: he was unconscious for 24 hours and caught a serious infection, which kept him in bed for weeks. Slowly, though, he got stronger, was released from hospital and in six months was living a more or less normal life.

Since then he has gone from strength to strength, running in five-kilometer road races, swimming, and teaching at the University of Pennsylvania Dental School. "There's nothing athletic I'd be afraid of tackling now," he says.

All that time he thought about the donor and his family. "I wrote a letter to them in my mind and every day I said it over to myself. But a fear of hurting them held me back."

Then one day, while driving with a man who had just agreed to buy his car, his heart chilled: he had just passed the end of Wharton Street. "I think my donor lived there," he said only half aloud. His companion's response took his breath away. "I was at his funeral. My wife worked with him."

Eagerly, though apprehensively, Gail's family and Larry's arranged to meet. They now think of each other as parts of an extended family. Gail joined the board of the Gift of Life Donor Program, the group that coordinated the donation, and has been a force in its multicultural activities ever since. Many times, she and Larry have given talks to increase public awareness of the need for more donated organs.

Why did she do it, she is often asked. "You have to help others, whoever they are or wherever they came from," she says, as though there could be no other possible answer. How did she feel about her boy's heart going to a white, not a black, man? It went to the person in greatest need, she replies. "The heart has no color."

Family Donates Five Kidneys – Three of Them to Strangers

A Midwest family has set a remarkable record in donation: five of its members have donated a kidney, three of them to complete strangers. They call themselves the One Kidney Club. United Network for Organ Sharing knows of no other family that can equal this achievement. The story began in 1990 when Aaron Schurman, then 17, was dying of kidney failure. His mother, Joan, did the only thing she knew to save him: she gave him one of her own kidneys. "It was wonderful to see him up and so pink" right after the operation, she says with a laugh.

For Joan herself, the process was much more painful. In the days before laparoscopic surgery, she spent five days in the hospital and for months afterward was unable to pick up her new grandson or drive the tractor on the family farm. But she was deeply grateful that she had

126

been able to save her son's life. He lived healthily for eight more years. Then, ominously, he began to see the first signs of the symptoms he'd had before. Slowly, his body began to reject the new organ.

For months, he kept it to himself. "I thought Mom would be crushed," he says now. But in time he became too ill to hide it. "He was a wreck. This young man looked as if he was going to die," Tom Falsey, Aaron's uncle by marriage, says. It got so bad that the doctors put Aaron back on dialysis, waiting for the day when a kidney would become available.

All this time Tom, then a 45-year-old project engineer, had been agonizing about what he could do to help. For a long while, a living donation didn't occur to him. "We weren't biologically related and I had the idea that matching in such cases was very rare, almost like winning the lottery."

But seeing Aaron's grey skin and the shuffling steps of an old man, he decided to at least find out. "You can't watch something like that and not do anything about it," he says. To his surprise, he was found to be a good match and, without hesitation, began to prepare – losing weight, exercising and, to be on the safe side, tidying up his financial affairs. "Then I felt guilty that I hadn't thought of it before," he says.

With Aaron rejecting his mother's transplanted kidney, the surgical staff made an educated guess. Thinking it would improve his opportunity to accept another transplant, they removed his failing kidney.

Things did not work out as planned. Forty-eight hours before the transplant was to take place, Tom was given a final cross match -- a routine check, he thought – but in those final hours the doctors decided the risk of rejection was too great and called off the transplant. He was dismayed. "I don't think you realize how much you want to donate to someone until you find you can't do it," he says. He had rarely been so downcast in his life.

Aaron's health continued to decline until his sister, Michelle, 33 at the time, and a mother of two young children, made a decision. Up to that point he had steadfastly refused to let her offer one of her kidneys. "I've taken enough from this family," he said. "How could I face your children if anything happens to you?" But now she insisted, and, after four years on the waiting list, he was too ill to talk her out of it.

The transplant was done five years ago and he now has a healthy life. "Something had to be done," Michelle says simply. "Time was running out."

Tom, by contrast, was still disheartened by his inability to help but an idea began to form in his mind that wouldn't go away. "While I was preparing, I'd learned just how serious the shortage of organs is and how people are dying on the waiting list. I came to see how urgent the need is for even one more kidney."

He was spurred on by the fact that there was no history of kidney disease in his own family. "The chances of me losing a kidney were very low -- too low to worry about when so many people are badly in need of something I can do without."

So it was that, without serious doubts, he decided to donate one of his kidneys to whomever on the waiting list The Nebraska Medical Center transplant team decided was the match in greatest need. Even as recently as 2003, that wasn't easy. Nebraska had no program for anonymous donors and had to set up new procedures. Tom had to answer a slew of questions – including some, he says, designed to make sure he was sane, and others that he knew a living donation involved the attendant risks of major surgery.

"By then, however, they could see how determined I was and, in the end, they agreed," he reports. The recipient turned out to be 16-year-old Jordan Shaw of Omaha, who had suffered from cancer since he was two years old and whose kidney function had been destroyed. No one in his family was a suitable donor.

As a freshman, Jordan missed 43 days of school because of dialysis and, when he had to make up the lost time, used to drive to the clinic at 5:30 am, three days a week, before going on to summer school. Understandably, one of the things he enjoys most nowadays is late night television. When he met Tom, he said he'd be grateful forever. "You can't really say thank you just once," he explained.

Tom himself came through the surgery without significant problems of any kind. "It was a little like having a cold. I had aches and pains, I was tired and couldn't sleep well. But that was all. There was never any suggestion of writhing in pain." He didn't even take the morphine the doctors had ordered for him.

The emotional impact was equally low-key. Tom's feelings on meeting Jordan were a mixture of thankfulness that he was doing so well and a worry that the kidney he had given was so much older than the recipient. "I kept hoping I'd taken good enough care of it so that he would have it for a long time," he remembers.

"I'd also learned that good matches between unrelated people are not that rare. In fact just about everyone's organs are a match for someone on those long waiting lists. I don't know why more people don't step forward."

That, however, was only the first chapter. Tom's brother Jim, a Catholic priest, was so impressed by the good that had resulted and how well Tom had withstood the surgery that he decided to follow suit.

It was now Tom's turn to worry. "Because it was a walk in the park for me, I didn't want him to think it was free of risks. 'It's not like giving blood,' I remember telling him."

But Jim was equally determined, the donation for him being also a religious experience, believing as he does that as custodians of God's gifts all of us have an obligation to use them to help others. "I had two functioning kidneys, someone else had none. The kidney I donated had served me well for 59 years."

His recipient was Karen Bryce, a single parent, who nine years earlier had given one of her own kidneys to her father and later found that her remaining kidney was failing. She looked so ill that her two teenage daughters thought she was going to die. She says she thinks of Jim every day. "I did it for someone I loved and I had no reservation. But to do it for a total stranger was beyond my comprehension." Only about 450, of the more than 84,000 living donor cases recorded by United Network for Organ Sharing since 1988, are from anonymous donors.

A few months later, Tom's wife, Joyce, impressed particularly by the difference a transplant has made to Aaron, her brother's son, decided to give one of her kidneys, too. "Before, he was so sick that he could hardly walk. A year later he looked great," she says. "You can't not react to that."

Her kidney changed the life of Regina McDonald, a 39-year-old factory worker who had been on dialysis for six years. "I saw people who died," she says. "I saw people who gave up. They didn't want to fight any more."

Now members of the One Kidney Club try to spread the message still more widely. But Tom says there is one point he can't make people understand. "If you are healthy enough, it's not that big of a deal. It's not heroic. There is, however, a sense of accomplishment, knowing that every day you've made a huge difference in someone's life."

Two Weeks a Citizen, Then Killed

Two weeks after she became a naturalized American citizen, Dereck Lopez, an accomplished and beautiful 18-year-old, who lived in Fort Worth, was killed by a drunk driver on her way to a family Halloween party. "We were so proud of her," says her father, Jorge. "We brought her to Texas from Mexico, when she was just three years old, and she never stopped working to make the most out of her life."

She went to college, was a teaching assistant in a bilingual program and was training to be a kindergarten teacher. She became a black belt in karate and tae kwon do and was on the junior Olympics team. She dreamed of representing the United States in the Olympics. In her last competition, she won gold medals.

But, more than that, says Jorge, ever since she was a small child she was always helping other people. "If ever someone needed something done, she was the one who would do it."

One night in September 2002, six weeks before she was killed, she came into her parents' room where they were watching a program from Mexico about organ donation for children. "If I could help those children by doing that, I would do it," she said.

During the six days she was in a coma, Jorge and his wife, Blanca, had time to think of all those things. But the number of people who felt close to her surprised even them. One night, says Jorge, 250 people came to the hospital. A drug company representative stopped their son, George, to say he'd never seen so many visitors there. "It must be someone important," he added. "It is someone important," George replied. "It's my sister."

So, on the sixth day, when they were told their daughter's brain showed no activity, Blanca had no hesitation in saying they wanted her to be a donor. "What about bone and tissue?" they were asked. Whatever can be used, they replied.

"The whole family agreed," Jorge says. So, apparently, did the whole community. "More than 700 people came to the memorial service – people of all races and all ages. The priest said we had done a great thing. That made a big impression on people who thought the Catholic Church was not in favor."

The Lopez family has become close to three of her five organ recipients. "After five years the lady who got her heart, who lives in North Carolina, still calls my wife almost every day," Jorge says.

To their surprise, the two men who got her kidneys already knew each other. Before the transplant they went to the same dialysis clinic. One is an African-American, who had been married 12 years but had no children. A year after the transplant, he became a father. The other, who is Hispanic, and was very frail, has now regained his strength and has since married.

"I never felt there was any difference between the races," says Jorge. "Now I know it. There is a part of Dereck in all those different people."

He and Blanca, neither of whom had ever done any public speaking, set up the Dereck Lopez Foundation and now talk to all types of Hispanic audiences, including a visit to the national transplant center in Mexico. They find little opposition to organ and tissue donation. "Sometimes somebody will say, 'I don't think the Church is in favor.' But we remind them of what was said at the memorial service." With Hispanics forming one-quarter of all people on the waiting list in the Fort Worth area, they know they are helping save lives.

Donation has also done something for Jorge. "When Dereck was killed, I was so angry. I was thinking such bad things. I might have gone on feeling like that. But I told myself I had to do something positive to put my feelings in the right way. The way she has helped all those people has helped me do that. The pain of losing her is there, but I'm not bitter anymore."

Fighting for Life in a Louisiana Storm

On Thursday, September 22, 2005, a mother and her young family in New Iberia, Louisiana, still pulling themselves together from Hurricane Katrina a month earlier, were evacuating yet again from their mobile home just ahead of a category four storm. They were going only 10 miles to Youngsville, which had not been ordered to evacuate. Crossing an intersection they were hit by an 18-wheel truck.

The mother, Christie Leger, and a friend escaped with minor injuries. But in the back seat, three-year-old Devan took the full impact. He was rushed to Lafayette General Medical Center with catastrophic head injuries.

Christie's husband, Roger, joined her there and both realized from the beginning the gravity of the situation. "We knew all along there was a strong chance he wouldn't make it," he says. "We felt so helpless just sitting there."

Almost unaware of the storm, the Legers remained at the hospital, while their son's life slowly ebbed away. On Saturday afternoon, they were told he was dead. They talked together for a few moments. Then, without being asked, they told the doctors they wanted to donate his organs.

"I kept thinking, suppose he needed a heart to save him, I'd be sitting on the edge of the bed hoping and praying that someone would donate," says Christie. "And then, I thought, someone is out there, sitting on the edge of a bed, and for them a heart really would save their child. How can we say no to helping them?"

Twenty-five miles away, Kallie Barras was helping move furniture in her grandmother's house to protect it from the rising flood water. Her job as first responder for LOPA, the Louisiana Organ Procurement Agency, included making the first contact with families about donation. She was not on call that day but, with power shutting down all over the area and roads blocked, she was asked to drive to Lafayette. She remembers the deserted and flooded streets in the town and the highways empty of traffic.

When she got to the hospital she learned that with the storm, named Rita, approaching fast, Devan was being transferred to Our Lady of the Lake Hospital in Baton Rouge, where his organs could be recovered. She also learned that the only ambulance available did not have a ventilator suitable for children. So, on the one-hour drive, she and one of the LOPA nurses, Vashaun Rodgers, took turns squeezing a bag of oxygen to keep Devan's blood flowing and the organs working.

The beating rain and winds of up to 120 miles per hour continued to wreak havoc, driving a wall of water from the Gulf of Mexico inland. Many staff members couldn't get to the hospital and, because of the curfew, those who were there were not allowed to leave. Telephones weren't working. The hospital lab was so overloaded that the routine blood tests to check a patient's potential to be a donor couldn't be done; information that would help place any donated organs couldn't be sent because the fax machines had shut down; and the major transplant centers in New Orleans were closed.

While the turmoil swirled around him, Devan was kept on a ventilator so that when conditions returned to normal his organs would still be viable for donation.

Slowly the storm abated, but it continued to determine the outcome. With the organ donation systems within the state disrupted, it was not possible to offer the organs to any Louisianan. Instead, they had to go to the top candidates outside the state. Transplant centers in three different states were called and surgical teams flew in through the now calm skies. Devan's heart went to a five-year-old from North Carolina, his liver to a one-year-old girl in Florida, his small intestine to an 18- month-old in New York, and both kidneys to a 63-year-old man in Florida.

Roger describes Devan as a playful, smiling, affectionate child. The mobile home seems empty without him, and his brother, Tyler, now nine, can't get used to the idea that he is no longer there to laugh and play with.

"But we've never had any regrets. If I had to do it all over again, I wouldn't change a thing," Christie says. "It all seemed so useless when he died. It has given us some peace of mind to know that it all hasn't happened for nothing."

Recipients Surprised by Their New Lives

Seven years ago, a young Kentucky man with no history of serious medical problems suddenly took ill, went into a coma and was given a new liver. The hospital staff congratulated themselves on saving his life. When he woke up and found he had received a transplant, he reacted with anger and rebellion. "No one gave me a choice," he said.

It turned out that family relations had been strained and he objected to someone he had quarreled with making such a fundamental decision for him. It says a lot about transplantation that when Phyllis Kaiser, a transplant coordinator at Jewish Hospital Transplant Center in Louisville, heard that story, she was only mildly surprised. "The reactions of recipients cover the whole spectrum," she says.

"Even before the operation, many people feel uneasy about waiting for someone to die so that they can live. Then when they get the new organ they sometimes feel they bear some responsibility for that death.

'I don't deserve this,' some of them say. In their minds they know it's absurd, but they find it hard to shake off the idea."

Sometime in the first six months, after the initial euphoria at getting the transplant wears off, many patients go into depression. They are taking strong medications, their thoughts are no longer fixed on the single goal of surviving and many are facing, after an interval, all of life's usual frustrations. "Why did I do this?," they ask themselves.

"But you should see them after 12 months," Phyllis says. "They are different people: enjoying being back in the world, participating in sports, being able to play a full role in family life. So we warn all transplant recipients that the surgery is only the first of the hurdles they will have to overcome. Most of them do overcome them and afterward wonder how they could have questioned the benefits."

Her first job with patients is to evaluate them to see if they are eligible to be on the transplant waiting list at all. A malignancy, even outside the diseased organ, might be enough to disqualify them.

"We prefer to see patients soon after the symptoms have started and are what we call 'medically early.' They are followed at three-month intervals -- or less if their condition deteriorates," Phyllis says. "Their chances are much better if they are referred to us before they become very sick."

Whatever their mood, the physical reality is that, after the transplant, all of them need to take immunosuppressant drugs. A large part of the coordinator's job is to ensure compliance.

"One patient we were all very fond of started smoking again after his liver transplant," Phyllis says. "He was diagnosed with lung cancer and we watched him deteriorate for a year and a half. The last time I saw him I gave him a hug and all I could feel were his ribs. Then he was dead. It's very frustrating, when the whole team has invested such effort and affection, to watch people do that to themselves."

There are plenty of scares even for less extreme cases. "We tell every patient that rejection episodes are likely. But whenever they hear the word 'rejection' they are understandably afraid. Their body's immune system is trying to force out the new organ and it appears to be winning. Luckily, cases of acute rejection can usually be treated with stronger medications until the rejection is under control. What we've got to avoid is chronic rejection, which is not reversible."

Some kidney patients who have repeat rejections have to go back on dialysis. "That's a blow to even the most optimistic ones and for some it's devastating. Some can go to their dialysis three days a week and still manage a full-time job. But others are so sick that it just wipes them out, so that they aren't able to do anything on the in-between days. Then it's time to go back on the machine again. They begin to wonder: what's the point? And some take themselves off dialysis knowing they will certainly die."

This is the downside, but Phyllis went into this job for a reason. Previously she worked for Kentucky Organ Donor Affiliates, asking bereaved families to donate. Nineteen years ago, she lost her own 18-year-old daughter, Kim, to a rare, aggressive form of ovarian cancer. After that, she felt the need to see the other side of transplantation.

Now, when she has a hard day, she remembers another 18-year-old who had been sick since birth and got a new liver. "All the nurses watched over her as though she were part of their own families. Today this woman, who had always had a restricted life, has a career, a husband – we all went to her wedding -- and a little boy, three things she never dreamed she would live to experience."

The successes, she can see for herself, far outweigh the failures. But there's even more. "Recipients in general go on to become productive members of society and, having seen so vividly someone else's selflessness, I think many of them become better people, too," she says. "That's a wonderful gain for the world."

Identical Twins, Identical Illness, Identical Transplants

Three days after Ana Stenzel was born in Hollywood in 1972, she was operated on to remove an intestinal blockage. The risks were high for so tiny a patient but the procedure was successful. The hospital staff, however, suspected a deeper cause. Tests showed that was so: Ana had cystic fibrosis, the killer that attacks the lungs and the digestive system.

Now the attention turned to Isa, her identical twin, who had shown no signs of problems but, since the disease is genetic, was at high risk, too. Her mother and father, one from Japan, the other from Germany, already shocked by Ana's condition, learned that Isa had also tested positive.

"This is a progressive disease," they were told. "The lungs will deteriorate and eventually fail. There is no cure."

Until they were five, the girls were treated with digestive enzymes and antibiotics to combat chronic coughs. After that, more drastic treatment was called for. For 45 minutes, twice a day, they lay on pillows while their parents paddled their chests and sides to dislodge the thick mucus that clogged their lungs and could cause a fatal infection. "Whenever we missed a day or two we got sick right away," Isa remembers.

As they grew older, the sessions increased – first to three a day, then to four, eventually a total of five hours a day. "The burden on our parents was enormous," they say, "but they never gave up." Each birthday the whole family made the same wish: "Please let there be a cure for cystic fibrosis."

From about their 12th year the girls took on some of the burden by taking turns to pound on each other's chest and by 18 they were doing it all themselves. "It took a huge slice out of every day," says Ana.

Throughout childhood, they were in and out of hospitals with lung infections, two or three weeks at a time. Both suffered from coughing spasms that doubled them up. Often they couldn't walk without continuously pausing for breath.

They thought and talked a lot about death. It was not fanciful. By the time they finished college, all four girls who had shared a cabin with them in a summer camp for children with cystic fibrosis had died.

Through all the distractions and fears, they remained active – the family did a lot of hiking and both girls were on the swim team at the local YMCA. "We couldn't keep up with our healthy friends but we did things within our abilities," they say. Both also found the will and courage to study hard enough to be accepted by Stanford University and later went on to earn master's degrees at the University of California-Berkeley.

From time to time, things seemed to get better for a while and Isa had enough confidence to get married. But underneath, the disease was progressing.

Ana had always been the sicker of the two. Often at night she would wake up in a panic fighting for breath. "I felt as though I was drowning," she explains. Nevertheless, she was shocked when, at age 24, tests showed she had only 30 percent of normal lung function. Her doctor put her on oxygen.

She was determined not to draw attention to herself by using her portable tank at her part-time job as a genetic counselor, although that decision brought on headaches, sweating and exhaustion. For the other 20 hours a day, she was dependent on it. "It made me feel better. I could go for simple walks again." It marked another depressing stage in her decline, however, and brought with it lurid thoughts of dying.

In March 1997, she agreed to be registered for a transplant, though with many doubts. "I knew that lungs were the least successful of all organ transplants. One of my closest friends – she was only 22 -- died after two failed lung transplants."

For the next three years she waited. Then, at 4 o'clock in the morning on June 14, 2000, her pager went off. Stanford Hospital & Clinics was telling her she was being offered a pair of lungs and she must come in immediately. In the shower, she was filled with both excitement and dread. "I kept thinking this might either be my last shower or my last shower with CF."

The surgery lasted nine hours. Her lungs were so diseased, she was told, that they were attached to the wall of the chest and had to be scraped off. But all went well enough that she was discharged in 12 days. "That's the shortest stay I've ever had in hospital," she observes. "For the first time in my life, I didn't have to think about my lungs. They just worked by themselves. I used to wake up in disbelief that life could be so easy and wonderful." She went on to climb, with her proud father, the famous Half Dome in Yosemite National Park, a 17-mile roundtrip and 5,000 feet up from the trailhead, carrying a 25 lb. backpack.

Isa, however, though still working part-time as a social worker in a hospital, was becoming increasingly dependent on oxygen, first two liters a day, then four, then ten. "Then one day I panicked because the oxygen equipment was no longer working. That day I decided I had to go back into the hospital," she says.

"I hated, hated, hated the thought of it, but I couldn't run the risk any longer. I was coughing up cupfuls of mucus. And I was getting very scared." Her doctor asked her if she wanted to go on a ventilator if things got worse. "The thought frightened me terribly. Once on a ventilator, most people with end-stage cystic fibrosis never get off it."

On February 4, 2004, she started to cough up blood and drifted in and out of consciousness. Her family, in-laws and friends gathered at the hospital for what seemed inevitable. Having been on the transplant list for only two weeks, her chances of getting lungs in time, even though she was critically ill, seemed almost non-existent.

Yet the next evening, the California Transplant Donor Network called Stanford to say they had lungs – "in perfect condition" -- which matched her blood type and size.

Her fate was now in the experienced hands of Dr. Bruce Reitz, who had performed the first successful heart-lung transplant in 1981 and Ana's transplant. But it was touch and go. Her blood vessels, thinned by the punishment they had endured since birth, bled copiously during the operation and she needed a massive 40 pints of blood. One lung at a time was removed -- she saw them later in the pathology lab and describes them as "brown-gray, extremely enlarged, bloody, pus-filled and disgusting" -- and the new lungs were sewn in.

"I was told there was no evidence of any functional lung tissue remaining in the old lungs," she adds. "I was just grateful they had worked so hard until their very last breath."

She can still scarcely believe how well she feels. "Without having to spend hours a day trying to free up my chest, everything is different. I've gone back to work, I can swim a hundred laps and hike ten miles. I've been cross-country skiing at 8,000 feet. For years, I was too short of breath to sing. Now I've joined a choir."

Neither twin forgets the donors who saved them. But, equally, neither of them has any doubts of the dangers that remain. If there had been any doubts, they would have been banished by a bout of rejection that hit Ana, severe enough to put her back on the waiting list. Yet, although gasping for breath with the least exertion and the familiar drowning sensation in the middle of the night, she went about her life with grace and an undimmed spirit. In July 2007, she got her reward: another pair of lungs.

Both women are profoundly grateful for the "wonderful years" transplantation has already given them. As Isa puts it, "I want everything I do to have a purpose. I feel my transplant was a form of resurrection. I want to be worthy of it."

Kidney Patients Rescued from Miserable Life

Sometimes in the middle of the night, the pager by Dr. Gabriel Danovitch's bedside will ring and a nurse will say something like this: "We've had a kidney offered for patient Rodriguez." It's a call he's been hoping for that could change the life of a 35-year-old diabetic, who has been on dialysis three days a week for three years, fatigued by even normal living, unable to concentrate enough to finish an article in the newspaper, and terrified that she might have to leave her young children without a mother.

But the call is not the simple solution he wanted. "It belonged to an 18-year-old who was in a catastrophic car accident and its function is impaired," the nurse adds. Danovitch, medical director of the kidney and pancreas transplantation program at the UCLA Medical Center, asks a few rapid questions. Both he and the nurse have done this many times.

After a moment or two, he makes a decision. "It's outside the parameters for her. We'll have to decline." He lies back in bed, knowing the Rodriguez family will have to wait for another day. "We can't use kidneys that can hurt people," Danovitch says. "Sometimes the risks of waiting are less than of going ahead. It's a very fine line, however, and a constant challenge to try to do the right thing."

An incident like this is emotionally draining for everyone involved. A little stronger patient or a little less damage to the new organ might have tipped the balance the other way. Judgment calls like that go with Danovitch's job. His pager is on virtually all the time, as it has been for more than 20 years.

At any time, he might be told of an impending brain death of someone with severe cancer or a history of drug addiction. "The kidneys may have deteriorated so much that it's doubtful we can use them," he explains. "We don't want to put the family through the pain of deciding if they want to donate if, in the end, we aren't going to take it. On the other hand, we desperately need every usable organ we can get. At times like that you are very conscious you have the fate of entire families in your hands."

Questions arise also about post-operative problems: patients whose bodies are making extra efforts to reject the transplanted organ, perhaps, or the occasional fever that would be treated routinely in a normal person but has to be watched intently in a recipient.

Danovitch has held his present position since 1983 and has been involved in literally thousands of transplant cases. When he started, the success rate was not much more than 50 percent. "We used to tell the patients just that: 'your chances are 50-50,'" he recalls. "Only the plucky went for it. Some did well and are still doing well. Some had to go back on dialysis, the process that replaces their defective kidneys in cleansing the blood. And some died. In those days, transplant wasn't that attractive an option."

All that changed with the advent of cyclosporine, one of the most powerful drugs in medicine, which fights the body's unremitting efforts to reject a foreign body. "It's hard to express how miraculous a change that was. The first 20 or so transplants we did after that all worked," Danovitch says, the awe still in his voice after all these years. "They all worked, all 20 of them."

Twenty more years have brought a host of other improvements, large and small, so that now, as he puts it, "success is normative." Now, he points out, one-year survival rates for kidney recipients are in the 90-95 percent range and five-year survival rates are approximately 80 percent.

UCLA is doing nearly 300 kidney and pancreas transplants a year, more than ever before. The gratification the medical team finds in each of them is as great as it was when the program was doing only a fraction of that. "To see the delight that patients, who have been ill for so long, take in recovering the simplest bodily functions is always a thrill," Danovitch says. "Someone who hasn't been able to pee for years suddenly has a bagful of urine. To healthy people it's something they don't think about. To the sick it's like being given a new life. They can't believe it's happening to them."

Success has come with a price. As transplantation becomes the operation of choice for more and more patients with kidney disease, the waiting list grows inexorably. Like everyone else in the transplant community, Danovitch feels frustrated by the shortage of organs and is energetically involved in programs to make the public aware of the need for transplantation and the good that can come signing up to be an organ and tissue donor.

In addition, he is strongly in favor of living donation. Having thought about it for years, he acknowledges the ethical issues, especially the pressures on the potential donor. "Obviously, this has to be a decision made without coercion," he says. But such is the shortage of deceased donor organs that, without a hefty increase in the number of living donors, he can see only a steadily growing waiting time.

It's true, he observes, that many patients do surprisingly well on dialysis, taking the treatment with stoicism or high spirits, depending on temperament and their general state of health. "They know it's keeping them alive and they are grateful."

For others, however, sicker or not so well-prepared emotionally, it is a prolonged state of uncertainty and depression, stretching into years, as they try to fit the immobilizing regimen -- three days a week, four hours a day -- into their lives without too much disruption to themselves or their families.

"Their emotions are constantly up and down. They generally feel washed out on the day they have dialysis; the next day they normally feel better; the day after they start to feel worse again as they approach the next session. They don't have any sense of well being," Danovitch says.

For some, the situation is worse still. "Patients who have been waiting five years, especially the older ones, aren't the same people they were when they were first listed. In that time a lot of bad things can happen to people with their medical history: many are diabetic and that may bring with it blindness or an amputation or other complications. Some have had heart attacks. They may deteriorate so far they aren't even candidates anymore."

Divorce rates, too, are very high for dialysis patients. "Typically, one partner is healthy and the other is always tired, can't travel, doesn't want to do anything. When the waiting time is so long, the strain on the marriage is often too much. In those cases, of course, the condition of the patient is generally wretched, the loss of family life piled on top of debilitation and the fear of death. Many find it hard just to go on living."

To Danovitch, broken marriages are one more reason for encouraging living donations. "When a spouse donates, not only does the recipient gain but the couple gains, too. There isn't only the gratitude for the gift, though that itself is immense, nor just the feeling of having done the right thing, which is also very powerful. In addition, with two healthy partners, the marriage is often rebuilt."

Even after a transplant, there are many surprises. One of Danovitch's patients, a high-flying attorney with a relaxed and confident manner in the courtroom, who was transplanted 15 years ago, has been absolutely stable all that time. Yet every three months, on the night before he has his regular check-up, he confesses he is a basket case. "Nothing has budged, the transplant is solid as a rock, but he can't sit still until he gets the result of the blood test. That comes in normal, as it always has, and he doesn't think about it again for another three months," Danovitch comments.

Keeping in touch with such people reminds him how much good has been done. "When I meet patients who had a transplant many years ago and see them graying, like me, it hits me afresh that they have been living a full life all that time, seeing their children grow up, getting on in their careers, involving themselves in whatever is important to them," he says.

"We need to stop from time to time and remind ourselves that we are taking the organs of people who died and making them work in other people. It's extraordinary and it doesn't become less extraordinary because we do so many of them."

Rina Morales, 38 years old, is one of Danovitch's patients whose marriage came apart. Bouts of sickness, money worries at no longer being able to hold down two jobs and fear of what all this might do to her young son transformed her once happy life. Luckily, through good sense on both sides, she and her former husband remain on good terms.

As a child, her only symptoms were occasional severe headaches. But in El Salvador, where she grew up in a poor family, never getting past third grade, "they don't take us to a doctor unless we're really, really sick." Married at 18, the first intimation of something more serious was a miscarriage. A second baby was born two months prematurely.

"Medication didn't help and the doctors told me my kidneys will die one day. I didn't know what they were talking about. I didn't have any idea what dialysis was. And I didn't want to know anything about any of it," she says.

But in the end, there was no choice. Five years of dialysis followed, made worse by a series of surgical procedures to deal with a tendency for her blood to clot. "My mother, who still lives in El Salvador, came with me to the clinic one day when she was visiting. It frightened her so much she couldn't stop crying – all those needles and poor old people. Some don't have an arm or a leg."

There were other concerns, less urgent, but always upsetting. Over the years, Bryan, that second baby, now 17, would ask her, "Can you help me with this or can we go to the store?" "Not today, honey," she found herself replying time and again, "I have to go to dialysis." Once a month she would call the hospital, always with the same question, but with a growing sense of desperation: "Do you know where I am on the list, please?" At home she prayed, "Please, God, give me a few more years. I need to be with my little boy."

For years, she struggled to stay at work, in the bookkeeping department of a laboratory. Then one day, when she was in the clinic, her cell phone went off. "This is Susan at UCLA," a voice said. "Can you guess why I'm calling?" "Yes," Rina thought, "I do. They've just seen that I've moved to a new address and now I'll have a lot of new forms to fill in." But, instead, the voice went on. "We've got a kidney for you. We want you to come in at 8:30 tonight."

"I was so excited. I couldn't believe it. But then I thought of something. 'Can I come in tomorrow morning?' I asked. 'I have to arrange for my son to stay with his daddy.'" No, she was told, you have to come in tonight. The new kidney would go in early the next day.

"Then Susan told me the donor was a 19-year-old, Hispanic like me, who had been killed in a car accident. I tried to imagine him and to think what his family was going through. And I also began to be scared."

As soon as she got home she sat down beside Bryan. "He was so thrilled. 'No more dialysis, Mom,' he said, 'never again?' Then I felt I had to say something I'd said to him when I first started dialysis. 'Listen, honey, everything will be okay but I have to tell you, just in case, if I don't come back to the house, you have your daddy to go to.'"

It was one of the hardest things she has ever had to say. "He was so shocked all he could say was, 'Momma, you're coming back to the house, aren't you? You are, aren't you?' So then I told him, 'Of course, I am. How could I leave you?' But when my boyfriend drove me to the hospital that night and Bryan got out of the car to go to his daddy's house, I thought, 'Will I ever see him again?'"

Everything went well, however. Her new life is like a dream. Her kidney function is excellent. "Color has come back to my face. My hair has a shine to it. There have been no complications at all. When people say, 'You look wonderful,' that's how I feel on the inside too."

The transplant gave her one more thing. With a whole new future to look forward to, Rina married again.

Transplant Consoles Lonely Brother

When Andrew Gryske and his older brother, Steve, lived on an old farm in Pewaukee, Wisconsin, they looked forward to their hard-fought, one-a-side basketball games in the barn. One evening in October 1994, Andrew, then 21, called Steve to say he was on his way home and was hoping to get in a couple of games before it got too late.

An hour later, he walked out to the silent barn and found his brother slumped on a couch, shot through the temple. He'd written a note, leaving things that were precious to him to his father and mother and his collection of antique "Popular Mechanics" to Andrew.

"We knew he suffered from depression for several years. He had been to several doctors and counselors and was on medications for it. But none of us had any idea that it would lead to suicide," Andrew says.

Barely alive, Steve was rushed to Waukesha Memorial Hospital, but soon all brain activity ceased. The loss for Andrew was crushing.

"Living in the country, we'd always depended on each other. He was my best friend and role model. I couldn't imagine life without him."

That day his father was traveling on business and couldn't be reached quickly enough to help make the decision about organ and tissue donation. It didn't affect the outcome. Steve, who had worked as a technician at the same hospital, had talked at home of the importance of donating. "The choice had already been made for my mother and me," Andrew says.

"We donated everything he could, all the major organs, tissue, bone and one cornea. When my father came into the hospital later that night and we told him what we'd decided, he said that's what he would have done."

As the lonely weeks wore on, however, Andrew began to have troubling questions. "I never doubted it was the right thing to do. But I often asked myself, 'Did we do any good? Was it worth it?'

"I couldn't visualize the people the organs went to. I didn't know what a recipient looked like. I knew what sick people looked like and I knew they had to be pretty sick to be on the list.

"I wondered if it was just somebody sitting up in a hospital bed and saying. 'I'm going to make it another six months.' Was it just prolonging a bedridden person's sickly life? Often it seemed to be so unimportant compared with losing Steve.

"About six months after he died, we started getting letters from some of his recipients telling us how ill they had been and how much better they were doing. It was good to hear. But I was still numb and couldn't really take it in.

"Then one day in October 1995, we found what we had been missing. We were all at my grandfather's house, doing some home repairs there, when a program blurb on CNN said an item was coming up about a man who ran a half marathon that he'd never expected to be in. His name was Kevin and he came from Seattle. Suddenly, we all felt certain this was one of the people who had written to us.

"And then, there he was on the screen, with two new lungs, running, not fast, but running 13 miles, simply because he could. That 60-second piece destroyed my preconceptions about donation. This wasn't a man in a wheelchair. It was someone making the absolute most of his second chance.

"I started to cry. A part of my brother just ran a half marathon, I thought. Steve, whose only exercise was basketball with me and who could scarcely even drive 13 miles without wanting to stop.

"We also heard from one of the kidney recipients, a woman who had been on dialysis for ten years, but managed to run a home for developmentally disabled children. One child came to her as a baby and she wanted to adopt him but her condition wouldn't allow her to. With her new kidney, she did adopt him and then expanded her house so she could take in more children. I began to think of the kids who now have a place to go because of Steve."

But even when the family was invited to the U.S. Transplant Games in Columbus, Ohio, Andrew expected to be among crutches and frail bodies. "I was amazed. I realized every one of the competitors would have died if someone hadn't donated. Yet here they were -- running, jumping, playing tennis and basketball.

"Most of all, I remember a ten-year-old boy in a swimming race. He was so far behind the others that most of them were out of the pool before he made the last turn. He was hardly moving. He looked so tired that he might just stop any time. It was hard to imagine he'd ever get there. Everyone was yelling for him. The noise was deafening. The closer he got to the finish, the louder it became and when he touched the wall you couldn't hear yourself think. It was the greatest moment in sports I've ever seen.

"Since then, I've never doubted the power of transplantation to transform lives."

"Perfectly Fit Man" Had Heart Failure

Approaching his 40th year, Jerry Prose, a major in the U.S. Army, took great pride in being in top shape, working out and running seven miles a day before reporting for duty at the Pentagon. One May morning in 1992 around 5:30 a.m., in the middle of his run, he began to feel short of breath but pressed on, expecting his second wind to kick in. The next moment he had the panicky sensation of being late for work, struggling to get out of bed and gasping for breath, with water pouring on his face. He had passed out, falling full length into the wet brush by the side of the trail.

The doctors said later that they thought he had gone into cardiac arrest and only the impact of the fall had started his heart up again. "I owe my life to a freak accident," he says.

At the time, a heart attack was the furthest thing from his mind. He picked himself up and ran the three miles back at the usual pace. In the changing room, he could see he needed to get the cuts on his hands and face attended to at the dispensary. After a few minutes there, one of the doctors asked, "How long have you had this irregular heart beat?"

He couldn't answer; he'd never had the slightest problem. But 10 days in Walter Reed Army Medical Center produced the information that his ejection fraction, a measure of the amount of blood being pumped by the heart, was 50 percent, compared with a norm of 55 to 75 percent. This was a surprise for a man as fit as he was but, being a born optimist, he decided the fall must be a fluke and he made no change in his running routine.

A year later he had another test. His ejection fraction was now 34 percent. "One day you're going to need a transplant," he was told. "That part didn't seem a big deal to me," he remembers. 'Okay, when it's time I'll get one,' I said. I was that naïve. I thought it was something like by-pass surgery: when you needed it you had it done."

Far more serious at the time was the shock that he was no longer healthy enough to meet the army's fitness standards. After 18 years in the service, and having never before fallen below the maximum level in the physical fitness test, he was medically discharged.

He and his wife, Helen, moved near Las Vegas, opening a small vending business and selling real estate, where he could be close to his parents. "I'd been away from home so long I hadn't seen much of them since high school and both of them were developing severe medical problems," he says.

Not feeling any discomfort, he continued to run four or five miles a day for another five years. Then one day, without warning, he collapsed again while running by the side of the road, breaking a wrist and knocking out some teeth. It turned out that his ejection fraction had dropped to the low 20s. "I knew now this wasn't something that would go away by wishful thinking or a good diet or hard exercise."

The doctors at the local hospital insisted on fitting him with a defibrillator, which was set at the highest shock level. "The first time it fired I'd been carrying some heavy filing cabinets. I began to feel light-headed and got down on my hands and knees. Then wham! I felt as if someone had just taken a baseball bat and slammed me in the chest. All the time I had that defibrillator, I never got used to it.

"Sometimes it would go off when other people were there -- once it was young nephews and nieces -- and I'd be on my knees, struggling to get up. It's an unnerving sensation. When it goes off, it's firing because at that very second you're dying. You're glad it's there, but you know it doesn't always work and it's only a matter of time before it doesn't shock you back to life. And all the time it reminded me how sick I was.

"Going anywhere was humiliating. My wife would be carrying the baggage and I'd be walking slowly behind her. It wasn't the role of a husband I wanted to play."

The transplant team at UCLA added him to the national waiting list in 1998. He was still on it when his daughter, Frani, was married early in 2000. He walked her down the aisle and then had to sit out the rest of the wedding. "I'm not even in the wedding photos," he says.

While Jerry wasn't working at all, Helen, a hospice nurse, would leave the house at 7:30 a.m. and get back at 9 p.m. "She prepared all my meals before she left and, for the whole day, I sat on the couch and never moved, except to go to the bathroom or let the dog out. I knew what time it was not so much by the clock but by what shows were on television. Any exertion could trigger the irregular rhythms. That's what my life had come down to.

"The diet was strict: small bland meals day after day, virtually no salt, no more than 64 ounces of fluid a day. You haven't lived until you've had soup without salt in it. It's like drinking bath water. My wife told me repeatedly she put patients into hospice who were in far better shape than I was.

"My mother tried to comfort me. At least you're alive, she said, even if it's just sitting on the couch. Though she was dying of cancer herself, I was still her little boy. It frightened her when I said I'd rather be dead."

At 1:30 a.m. on a drenching night, the phone in the bedroom rang. Jerry woke with a start and was shocked to see the hall light was still on. That meant their 19-year-old son, Sean, was still out. He saw vividly the wrecked car in the pouring rain, the ambulance with its lights flashing, the police.

Helen picked up the phone and let out a cry. She handed it to him without a word. Deathly afraid, he heard a voice he didn't know say, "Is this Mr. Prose?" He waited for her to say, "This is the police department." Instead, she told him, "We have a heart for you."

"Now I was so excited I began to worry that my defibrillator would fire and knock me down. But it didn't go off and we climbed into a tiny air ambulance we'd booked ahead of time and flew to Los Angeles through the thunderstorms, taking far longer than we expected.

"You're always aware that for a transplant someone else must die suddenly for you to live. But it wasn't till then that it really hit me. Don't get me wrong. I wanted that heart very badly. But I was overwhelmed at the thought of what must have happened for me to get it. And I thought of someone getting a call in the middle of the night and how frightened I had been just an hour before that we might have lost our own son."

At the UCLA Medical Center, time was slipping away. The heart had come from Colorado, close to the maximum limit at which it could be kept viable. Jerry just had time to ask one of the surgeons,

"Can you tell me anything about the donor?" "I can only tell you this," he replied. "It belonged to a 19-year-old boy."

When he woke he heard the heart monitor which had previously been racing irregularly now giving off a gloriously steady 'beep… beep…beep.' His hands and feet felt warm for the first time in years. He wanted to sing. Seven days later he walked out of the hospital into the warm sunshine. "It was only then that I realized how much my life had changed."

After seven weeks he ran a mile. Since then he has never had any significant problem and works out as hard as he ever did. Last year, he took up a new sport and is now certified as a master scuba diver.

He knows there are risks in a transplanted heart but says, "I've already seen so many things I would have missed: our children growing and being successful, grandchildren born and the thrill of being alive every new day. My mother slowly died but I was able to be with her all that time. She was so happy to know I was myself again."

Basketball Champion While in Need of a Transplant

Sean Elliott's three-pointer, when the San Antonio Spurs trailed the Portland Trail Blazers by two points with 9.9 seconds to go in the 1999 NBA playoffs, is one of those moments in sports that no fan who saw it will ever forget. Catching a hard pass that nearly threw him off balance, swiveling almost out of bounds with scarcely time to set himself and the ball flying straight to its target instantly became the Memorial Day Miracle. But even more miraculous was that he did it while in the later stages of kidney failure.

He then played two more games to help Spurs win the Western Conference and another five against the New York Knicks to win the championship. In all these games he played with the grace and explosive power that stamped his career. Asked how he managed it, he says simply, "I love the game. Until that season was over, I threw the transplant into the back seat."

Remarkably, he had been suffering from kidney disease for six years. He first suspected something was wrong at the end of the 1993 season. "I felt weak and lethargic. At first I thought I was just stressed but then it became obvious that I was retaining water in my body. Every morning when I woke up my hands and face were swollen and, when I pressed on my shins, I could see the imprint of my fingers for a minute afterward."

Over the years he had a battery of tests, which confirmed that his kidneys were failing and that in all likelihood he would need a transplant. But he continued to push himself as hard as ever. In the 1998-99 season he started in all 50 games, scoring double figures in 32 of them and his 10,000th career point.

"I wasn't going to let anything get in my way," he says. "I've always been like that. When I was 13, I tore my knee badly enough that my doctor told me he didn't believe I'd ever play basketball again. But when he took the cast off one Monday, I was playing at the YMCA on Saturday."

Determination and medication saw him through the 1990s but his kidneys were steadily deteriorating. He remembers falling after colliding with Kobe Bryant of the Los Angeles Lakers in the round before the Portland game. "I felt so exhausted I could scarcely pick myself up," he says. "I just wanted to lie there."

But after the final Knicks game it was clear that something would have to be done soon. For the first time Sean told his family how serious things were. His father, mother and both brothers all offered to be donors though, in the end, only his mother and one brother, Noel, a year and a half older than Sean, were eligible. "She would have done anything to help but Noel insisted it should be him. Several times he told me he felt that's what he was here to do," Sean says.

In August 1999, the transplant was done, without incident at first. But after a few days a leak developed between the new kidney and the bladder. "The pain was one of the worst things I've ever experienced," he says. A second procedure was done to correct the problem. This time there were no complications.

"The difference in how I felt compared with the last year was as though someone had flicked the light on," he remembers. "I was out of the hospital in ten days, walking upstairs as soon as I got home. 'I want to play basketball again,'" I told the doctor. 'The only thing that can stop you is you,' he said."

Seven months after the transplant, in March 2000, Sean played again for the Spurs, the first player in league history to come back after a major organ transplant. "I felt terrific. The only thing that held me back was that I hadn't been to training camp. But the following season I was almost back to normal. I had a lot of stamina. I had my legs back. I thought I could play for another three or four years."

As it turned out, however, he was dogged by shoulder and knee injuries. "One day I came back after sitting out for a few games and I just wasn't the same. This time, it didn't get better. I could have continued to play, but I didn't want to go on like that." He retired in 2001 at the age of 33 and began broadcasting games for the Spurs. Still full of energy, he works out three or four times a week, plays golf and speaks on behalf of organ donation.

"I want people to know they can make it. 'You can overcome the odds,' I tell them and, 'You don't have to let sickness get in the way of what you want to do.' And I tell them about Noel, who's healthy, happy and has had three children since he gave me his kidney. If you saw us together and didn't know our story, you wouldn't have any idea that anything unusual had happened."

As for the Memorial Day Miracle, Sean says it wasn't as surprising as it seemed. "In the huddle, I told the guys, 'I think I have another three-pointer in me.' When I caught the ball and faced the basket, I didn't think I had much choice. In fact, I felt I couldn't miss. I was excited, of course, but mainly because we'd won. It was only afterward when I got in my car and my cell phone was full of missed calls, some from people I hadn't seen in years, that I realized what a big thing it was."

The Man Who Donated Twice

Fourteen years ago, Dr. Kenneth Moritsugu, then an assistant surgeon general of the United States, was driving back to his home in Washington, D.C., from a day of taking his aunt and sister sightseeing in Baltimore, when the traffic on Route 29 began to slow down. At first he thought it was just one of the usual buildups on this busy road. But then as the traffic slowed to a crawl, he remarked casually to his passengers, "It looks as though there's been an accident."

As his car inched forward, he saw a cream-colored Honda that had evidently been struck broadside as it had made a left-hand turn, perched on the top of a small rise by the side of the road. He recognized it instantly: his own family car, which only his wife, Donna Lee, could have been driving that day. "I tried and tried to deny it, but I couldn't," he recalls.

He pulled in as close to the accident as he could, despite impatient police signals to keep on moving. By the time he could run up to explain, the ambulance had driven off, taking his wife to the nearby Holy Cross Hospital. "She's been injured. We can't tell you anymore," the police told him.

"Everything that happened after that remains perfectly clear in my mind, every detail," Ken says, "and through it all there was the feeling that everything in my universe that had been in order was now adrift."

One thing he remembers is that the hospital staff did everything they could do to care for him and his family. Small things that to him made all the difference, like being put in a quiet room, where he could sit and make phone calls, and the nurse coming in to tell him of even minor developments: "she's in the emergency room" ... "the chief neurologist has arrived."

The calls he had to make to his two daughters, Erika (20) and Vikki (18), both away at college but not together, were searing. To them he tried to hold out some hope, though by then he knew there was precious little and, in fact, quite soon the chief surgeon came into the quiet room and told him his wife, just 45 years old, was dead.

He asked to see her. "They're cleaning her wounds," the nurse told him, "but I'll take you to her as soon as she's ready." The shock when he saw her was numbing. "The last time I saw her, just a few hours before, she was so vibrant and vivacious. Now she was so still."

Uppermost in his mind by then was the emptiness facing him and his girls. "I'd never had to deal with that kind of tragedy before. We don't get any training in how to behave." But as the neurosurgeon walked with him out of the hospital and asked gently, "What would you like to do?" he suddenly recalled a conversation Donna and he had had years before, when she had reminded him she had signed her donor card and added, with a conviction that stayed in his mind, "I want to give my body to science."

Ten years older than his wife, it had never occurred to him that he would be called on to make that decision. Now, helped also by the way the hospital staff had cared for him, the way forward was clear. He told the surgeon he wanted to donate Donna's organs and tissues. Like so many others, he found consolation in the thought that in one decision, he was both carrying out her dying wish and helping anguished families waiting for a transplant.

For most donor families, that moment is a watershed, but for him it was only part of the process. Four years later his daughter, Vikki, who was an insulin-dependent diabetic, fell into a coma. It lasted several weeks and left her with the mentality of a six-year-old. Ken arranged for her care in an assisted-living home, where she could be looked after, around the clock if necessary. One evening, around 7 o'clock, his telephone rang. It was the administrator at the facility, telling him that Vikki had broken free from the rehabilitation home. But that was only part of the message, which went on, "She was hit by a car while crossing a street. We don't know how badly. They're taking her to the trauma center now."

Scarcely pausing, he jumped into the car. When he arrived, she was still on her way and no one could tell him if the accident was serious or not. Sometime after eight he sensed, rather than heard, the beat of helicopter blades. "They're bringing in a young woman now," the nurse on duty told him. "Is it my daughter?" "I don't know," she replied. "This is a Jane Doe."

More waiting followed until, frantic with worry, Ken pushed his way into the emergency room and there, inert and damaged beyond repair, was Vikki, 22 years old. Three days later, she was pronounced dead. "You try to find some sense of stability but feel only the total loss of any ground under you," he explains.

Far from being easier to decide about organ donation, this time it was more difficult. "My mind was in turmoil. I didn't know what she would have wanted. We'd never talked about it. Just summoning up the energy to consider the decision, knowing there's nothing you or anyone else can do for your daughter, was almost more than I could do."

Meanwhile, he had contacted his first wife, Sandy, Vikki's mother, who flew 16 hours from her home in Hawaii. Together they made the decision to say yes. Like Donna, Vikki's organs went to four people, her corneas to two others and bone and skin grafts to many others. Only later did he find out from Erika that the two girls had talked about it and decided that, if something should happen to one of them, that's what they would want to do.

Ken, too, is "absolutely sure" this decision, like that for Donna, was the right one. He concluded this without meeting any of the recipients from the two donations. "I didn't feel I needed to meet them. It was enough for me that they'd been helped." Instead he sees it as having put something in the pool from which those who are in greatest need can benefit. "Every time I see a recipient, I feel so glad we put in our contribution," he says.

One of his wife's recipients was a retired police officer in Florida, who had suffered for years from coronary artery and congestive heart disease. By the time Donna died, he was close to death himself. Then he received her heart and went back to work as a private detective.

Seven years later he died from an unrelated condition. Until the end, his donated heart was reported to be "doing fine." Later Ken met his widow, Carol, who told him how grateful she was for those seven years. "We have Donna's picture along with the rest of the family pictures. It's still there and always will be," she said.

Ken's life has taken a different turn. As the deputy surgeon general, and second highest-ranking public health physician in the United States, and subsequently the acting surgeon general, he became his department's spokesman for organ and tissue donation and has gained international recognition for his work in raising awareness of the shortage.

His life no longer has the loneliness it once had. Seven years ago he married Lisa Kory, a former transplant coordinator and executive director of TRIO, the Transplant Recipients International Organization. Two years later they had a baby, Emily Renee.

Over the years he has traveled incessantly, trying to make everyone he comes in contact with more familiar with the idea of donation so that, however unexpectedly a tragedy happens, from the back of their minds they may recall the positive feelings they had before they were struck down with grief.

In speeches he uses an expression that has become part of the transplant community's vocabulary: donor families, he says, are "ordinary people doing extraordinary things." It's clear to many others, however, that Ken Moritsugu is an extraordinary man doing extraordinary things.

Police Officer, Left for Dead, Golfing Again

For Mike Blood, November 16, 2000, began like many other days in his 29 years on the police force of the small Minnesota town of Edina: roll call at 6:30; a rundown on the previous day's activities; a walk over to his squad car just before seven. He expected to give out the usual number of tickets for minor offenses, help with car accidents, perhaps respond to a call about a shoplifting or someone having a heart attack. Always there would be a lot of reports to complete.

His heart was warmed, however, at the thought that he now had only 29 working days to go before retiring. He let his mind play on the fishing he would do and staying in bed on cold mornings.

This was not to be a normal day, however. Just before 10 o'clock he got a call on his car radio, saying a bank robbery was in progress downtown by a man armed with a handgun. "We had five officers on duty. When that kind of a call comes in everyone responds, but I was nearest, just a mile and a half from the bank," he recalls.

"At times like that, what I don't want to happen is to drive over to the bank, have the robber see the squad car and go back inside and take hostages. What I was looking for was where he would park his car. I knew he wouldn't want to come out of the bank and have to cross six lanes of traffic on France Avenue. And he wouldn't have left his car so that he could be seen getting into it by people watching from the bank.

"There's a parking lot on a side street, close to the bank, with a building that would be between him and the bank. It seemed like a good bet.

"The bank officer who had reported the robbery was using his cell phone, which meant that the robber wouldn't have seen any of the bank telephone lines light up. So, with luck, he wouldn't know we'd been alerted.

"In the parking lot, I found what I was looking for, a green Ford Explorer without license plates. I looked inside and saw a pile of guns and ammunition on the driver's side floor. Later it turned out there were seven guns and 2,000 rounds of ammunition. I pulled my gun out and over the radio gave a description of the vehicle to the dispatcher.

"I got into my car, planning to put it out of sight and wait for another squad car to arrive so we could confront the suspect together, away from other people.

"As I backed up, another message came in over the radio: 'The robber is just going out of the back door.' I knew I'd have to hurry. But before I could move, a man suddenly stood up between two parked cars, ten or 15 feet away, and from under his coat brought out an assault rifle."

Mike knew about guns like that. They fire 30 rounds at high speed and are powerful enough to go through a bulletproof vest. Sometimes they use bullets covered with Teflon, which break up into small pieces, like a shotgun blast, if they hit anything hard. They are known as cop killers.

"Before I could move the robber fired two shots, which went through the car window, hitting me in my right hip, passing through my body and coming out by the left hip. If I stayed in the car, I knew I was going to be dead. I threw the door open and scrambled to the back of the car, ducking down."

The robber came around the front of the car, continuing to shoot. Later investigators counted 18 bullet holes in the squad car. One of the bullets hit the windshield, went through the back window and hit Mike in the right leg, shattering six inches of bone and blowing away 50 percent of the calf muscle.

"I fell forward, hitting a nerve in my right shoulder so that I couldn't get to my gun. I didn't move that arm for three months. My only hope was to play dead. I took a deep breath and stayed perfectly still.

"People watching from nearby offices said later they saw the robber walk to the back of the car and fire two more shots into my back. I remember my body bouncing as they hit. Those shots went through me, through my abdomen mostly, broke up and took out two ribs. I didn't know it at the time, but I had a hole in my back big enough that you could stick your hand in.

"Moments later, I heard the sound of a car starting up and driving away. I had my portable radio in my left hand and I brought it up to my mouth and said the words I'd been taught but never before used in this quiet town, 'Officer hit, officer hit'; and gave a description of the car again."

At that moment, Bill Moir, another patrol officer, turned into the parking lot, saw the suspect pulling away and went after him. Just about the same time a man, who had been shoveling snow in front of his house and heard the pop-pop sounds of the shooting, thinking it might be an electrical problem with the squad car, came over to help. Mike was able to tell him where his oxygen canister was.

Moments later, Shelby Lane, another officer, who was on her first day alone on patrol, turned into the parking lot. She looked at the gaping bullet holes and put her fist in one of them to try to stop the bleeding. She asked the man who had come to help to do the same with another hole.

Meanwhile, the robber had stopped in the middle of the road and fired seven more times, cutting Bill Moir with flying glass and disabling his car. Then he jumped back into the car and took off, by now pursued by two other squad cars. At top speed he misjudged an intersection, hit the curb and blew out a tire. He got out of the car and leveled the rifle at the officers closing in on him.

Instead of an explosion, there was a click and everyone there suddenly realized he was out of ammunition. As he reached for another magazine, one of the officers shot him in the head. He turned out to be a 31-year-old who had lived by robbing banks since he got out of high school and was on the "wanted list" in states across the country.

Mike, still conscious, was rushed to Hennepin County Medical Center, where he stayed for the next ten months. In that time he had 19 operations and was given 120 units of blood. "So many pieces of those bullets were bouncing around inside me," he says. "I had holes in my intestines, a lot of tissue was cut up and a lot of organs were nicked. The hospital did a lot of innovative things to keep me alive."

Among other things, the doctors inserted a titanium rod in his right leg, screwed in at the ankle and knee. That saved the leg but more was needed. Three months later they put bone filler, from one of the 20,000 families who donate bone every year, into the six-inch hole in Mike's own bone. "Normally they would have taken bone from my hips, but there wasn't enough left for them to work with," he explains.

Eventually the transplant grew and filled out until it became part of his own leg. In time, the rod came out. Until then, Mike couldn't take a normal step. Now he can walk again, not perfectly, because his Achilles tendon was shot away, but enough to play 36 holes of golf and catch 100-pound halibut in Alaska. "I bless that donor every day," he says. Now he speaks at blood centers, Red Cross meetings and donor ceremonies.

He can't return to a completely normal life. His leg swells painfully if he doesn't rest it from time to time; he walks with a roll and reckons he spends two more hours a day than he used to just coping with the routine of dressing and moving around.

But it's been more than two years since his last operation and he is fit enough to work full-time. He has a loving family and has received 4,000 cards and letters commending him and praying for his recovery. "I think of myself as a very lucky man," he says.

You're Never Too Old

Recently, the liver of a 92-year-old New York man was transplanted into a 62- year-old woman. This was an exceptional case, but last year 12 organ donors in the New York area were more than 80 years old and 36 were between 70 and 80. Together, they accounted for 15 percent of all donors in the area.

"If we approach the families of elderly people about donation, they are almost always amazed," says Margaret Gallagher, hospital services manager at New York Organ Donor Network. "'Can you really use them? She was old, you know,' they say to us. But when they see we're serious, they are usually very willing. It's something most of them had never considered. Now they have something that can give them comfort."

The same surprise, she says, is evident among the older people that the organ donor group reaches out to in its education programs.

"'Nobody would want anything of mine,' they say. 'It wouldn't do them any good.' We hear this all the time. But when they realize they might be able to save lives, they are cheered at the thought that they can still do something that important.

"With people living longer, there are both more elderly potential donors and more potential recipients. Ten or 15 years ago, transplantation wasn't an option for patients in their 60s. Now it's routine," Margaret points out. "We are perpetually short of donated organs."

But that is only part of the difficulty. Even when a family has consented to a donation, in a metropolitan area such as New York unexpected obstacles can crop up at any time. "In a busy trauma center the operating room that we have scheduled for a recovery may turn out to be full all night as emergency patients are brought in," Margaret says. "Then we have to keep the deceased donor stable until the next morning. The delay can be very hard on the family.

"Sometimes the planes bringing in the surgeons who will recover the organs are held up because the airport is backed up. Time and again, we'll get a call from an ambulance carrying organs for a recipient saying it is stuck in traffic."

In one case that became famous, a former Buffalo Bills fullback, Doug Goodwin, waiting in New York-Presbyterian Hospital in Manhattan, was told late one night in 2001 that the heart he needed would arrive the next morning from Boston. That next morning was September 11. When the chartered plane carrying the heart left Logan Airport, it was on the same runway and just nine minutes ahead of American Flight 11.

The small plane landed at Teterboro Airport, New Jersey, and the heart was transferred to an emergency vehicle just ten minutes before American 11 exploded into the World Trade Center's North Tower. By the time the vehicle reached the George Washington Bridge, it was closed to all traffic. There was no other way to get across the Hudson River.

As the minutes ticked by, all the elements in the elaborate transplantation procedure were in full swing. The medical team was assembling, the operating room equipment had been checked and the patient had already been prepared for surgery. But the heart, packed in ice, and the surgeons who had recovered it, were backed up in a chaotic mass of traffic. But just when all seemed lost, the ambulance was allowed through, one of the last vehicles to enter New York that day, and the heart of a 48-year-old man saved Doug Goodwin's life.

"It takes many people to make a donation happen," Margaret says. "Everything has to fall into place: the referral to us from hospitals that might have only one brain death a year, all the testing that's needed, the coordination of surgical teams coming in from different parts of the country, the support we offer to families in shock, and much else. The potential recipients also have to be found and brought into the hospital or, if they are already in hospital and deteriorating, kept going on a ventilator for a few crucial hours longer."

With New York's diverse population, even getting consent presents unusual problems, among others that the next of kin, whose permission is needed for a transplant, may live in any corner of the world.

"We have to reach those people – sometimes in China or Russia, very often in Latin America. Sometimes they have no telephone at home. Often we need an interpreter. Sometimes the first they know that their loved one is dead is when we tell them. To them we're just a voice on a telephone. It can be an ordeal for everyone. Yet, even in conditions as difficult as that some people still say 'yes.' It's amazing, isn't it?"

Patches of Love: The Donor Quilt

After nine years Maggie Coolican has just laid down her sewing needle on a project that arose out of a searing tragedy and grew into an inspiration for thousands of people around the world.

In 1983, Maggie's youngest child, Katie, aged six and apparently in perfect health, was suddenly struck down in her school playground by a fatal brain hemorrhage. Despite the numbing grief, Maggie and her husband, Don, found the will and spirit to donate her organs and corneas. In death, little Katie Coolican saved lives, including one seven-year-old and one man who had been on dialysis Katie's entire life.

But Maggie wanted to do more. She wanted to honor and, in some way, ease the pain of families like her own. Then one day, sitting in the family car and doing what she habitually did on long journeys – sewing – the idea suddenly came to her: "Why not ask donor families to send in squares to make into a quilt?" Once she'd thought of it, she couldn't get it out of her mind.

Working through the National Kidney Foundation, she contacted families across the country. Many never responded. Some thought it a crass idea. But enough of them were enthusiastic, and some overjoyed, that she threw herself into it. It helped that she was following in a long and revered tradition of turning to quilting to soothe grief.

Now, instead of one quilt, there are 32, each with 70 squares, and she has stitched them all. Together they are a treasure trove of the most poignant memories of those 2,240 families.

Each square is a separate love story and, devastatingly, many of them are for children. One is part of a baby's blanket, another a picture of a child holding a baseball bat. There are pieces of T-shirts, a little boy's pajamas, a christening gown.

Some of the clothing is old, recalling for the family perhaps dozens of different occasions when it was worn. Some bear marks of repairs, evidence of some minor accident that would otherwise be long forgotten but has now been immortalized.

A few squares bravely manage a touch of humor, but the crushing grief in most of them is all too clear. One little face peeps out of a square, radiant with the joy of life, but accompanied by the chilling footnote: 1982-93.

Some are elaborate designs crowded with images of a fishing pole, baseball bat and football, with names and dates and perhaps a photograph, as though the family wanted to cram in every possible detail of a full life. Others are sparse and anonymous, as if to say 'we don't need any props to remind ourselves how much we miss you'.

The quilts travel to hospitals, schools and churches around the United States and to special events abroad, breathing life into grim medical statistics and reminding those who see them that behind every donation is a life that was snuffed out and a family that has had to overcome a staggering blow.

So effective has the idea been that now organ procurement organizations and tissue banks across the United States have their own local quilts. Year after year, they are cited as one of the most widely recognized symbols of organ and tissue donation. Versions for children have been started so they, too, can remember parents or siblings in a way that hopefully helps them come to terms with death.

Now Maggie has decided that, with 14 grandchildren, a full-time job as a donor family services coordinator and continued involvement in the National Donor Family Council, which she helped found, it was time to turn the bittersweet task over to someone else. "Life won't be the same without it," she says. "When I'm stitching a square I feel I'm part of that life. I ask myself if this little boy had a bicycle or if this girl liked reading."

She is still awed, she says, by the willingness of people to trust some of their most precious possessions to a stranger. "How can you treat something like that with anything less than reverence?"

Her last job was a square of such tender significance that she was unable to work on it until the end: Katie's. It is a simple patch, the face of a little girl who wanted to be a mud wrestler, the picture of young life with everything to look forward to.

It could have ended there, a senseless tragedy with consequences only for her grieving family. Instead, several families were saved from devastation and thousands more were made aware of the power of transplantation. Katie's death has done one more thing: it has inspired a work of art that is unforgettable.

The Boy Who Saved Thousands of Lives

The Author's Own Story

On the night my seven-year-old son, Nicholas, was shot we were playing a game in the car as we drove on vacation along the main road in Southern Italy between Naples and Sicily. As usual, he was hard to beat. I went over again the answers he'd given: the man I was looking for was a hero, a real person and we'd been to places where he'd lived. He wasn't American or British, not French or Roman or Greek. In the end I had no choice. "I give up," I told him.

"Bonnie Prince Charlie," said Nicholas happily. "You said he wasn't British," I protested. "No, I said he wasn't English," he answered. It was true. That's what he had said. This last win was typical of the way he did everything: he chose well, never cheated and had a lot of fun doing it. His teacher said he was the most giving child she had ever known and she always knew he was her teacher.

Soon he was asleep, propped up on the back seat next to his sister, four-year-old Eleanor, and I, driving beside my wife, Maggie, probably thought as I often did: "How can anyone be this happy?"

An hour or so later I had the first faint tremor of anxiety. A car, headlights on but dark inside, came up close behind us and stayed there for a few moments, unusual in Italy where cars generally pull out a long way behind and streak by. "There's something wrong," I said, half to myself. Maggie, who was dozing, sat up quickly.

Just then the other car moved out and began to overtake. I relaxed, nothing wrong after all. But, instead of overtaking, the car ran alongside us for a few seconds and through the night we heard loud, angry, savage cries – the words indistinguishable but clearly telling us to stop.

It seemed to me that if we did stop we would be completely at their mercy. So instead I accelerated. They accelerated too. I floored the car, they floored theirs and the two cars raced alongside each other at top speed through the night.

A few seconds later, any illusions that this was just a reckless prank vanished, as a bullet shattered the window where the two children were sleeping. Maggie turned around to make sure they were safe. Both appeared to be sleeping peacefully. It seemed like a blessing at the time. A second or two later, the driver's window was blown in and how that bullet missed both Maggie and me in the front seat we'll never know.

But by now, we were beginning to pull away and, from seeing them alongside, I watched them through the side mirror and then, falling further behind, the driving mirror, finally disappearing into the night. It turned out later that they had mistaken our rental car, with its Rome license plates, for another that was delivering jewelry to stores. We raced on, looking for somewhere with lights and people.

As it happened, there had been an accident on the road and an ambulance and police were already there. I stopped the car and got out. The interior light came on but Nicholas didn't move. I looked closer and saw his tongue was sticking out slightly and there was a trace of vomit on his chin. For the first time we realized something terrible had happened.

He was whisked away in the ambulance and, after answering questions from the police, we followed, with that feeling of gnawing emptiness that for months afterward never went away. In time we reached a small hospital, in the car park of which was an ambulance and, standing around it in total silence, what looked like the entire medical staff.

I hoped against hope that it was there for a different purpose but, when I looked inside, I saw Nicholas' pale face, peaceful and freshly washed, looking as though he had just been put to bed. The chief surgeon explained that he was too badly injured for them to operate and he would be taken to a larger hospital in Messina, Sicily, to see what they could do. I have never known such bleakness.

Two hours later, at the new hospital, the signs were ominous from the beginning. We were directed to a department called 'rianimazione' -- literally reanimation – and shown into a room, where again it seemed as though the whole medical staff was gathered and all again totally silent. After a moment, the chief neurologist said quietly, "The situation is very dramatic" and all the small shoots of hope that had grown in those two hours withered away. The bullet had lodged at the base of the brain, they told us, the seat of all brain functions, and he was too weak for them to operate. The only hope was that he might regain enough strength for them to try something later.

But, instead, his life quietly drained away. In death, as in life, he was no trouble to anyone. After two days all brain activity ceased and all the brightly-colored dreams of a young idealist, who had planned to do such deeds as the world has never known, died too.

For a while, Maggie and I sat silently, holding hands, and trying to absorb the finality of it all. I remember thinking, "How am I going to get through the rest of my life without him?" Never to run my fingers through his hair again, never to hear him say, "Goodnight, Daddy."

Then one of us — we don't remember who but, knowing her, I feel sure it was Maggie — said, "Now that he's gone, shouldn't we donate the organs?" The other one said "yes," and that's all there was to it. It was just so obvious: he didn't need that body anymore.

As it turned out, there were seven recipients, four of them teenagers and two others the parents of young children. One, Andrea, was a boy of 15 who had had five operations on his heart, all of which had failed. By now, he could scarcely walk to the door of his apartment. Domenica had never seen her baby's face clearly. Francesco, a keen sportsman, could no longer see his children play games. Two of the teenagers, Anna-Maria and Tino, had been hooked up to dialysis machines for years to ward off kidney failure, four hours a day, three days a week, losing their entire childhood, never being able to go far from home and already aware that they might never become adults. Silvia was a diabetic who was going blind, had been in multiple comas and couldn't walk without help. Finally, there was a vivacious 19-year old girl, Maria Pia, who on that very day was in her final coma from liver failure. Her brother had died of a liver disease, her mother was dead, too, and the family was preparing to take another devastating blow.

In that hushed hospital room in Messina these people were just statistics to us. But now, having met them and seen the agony they had gone through and knowing what would have happened to them, I don't think that Maggie and I could ever have looked back without a deep sense of shame, if we had shrugged off their problems as none of our concern,

Our decision, however, electrified Italy. The prime minister and president asked to see us, we were flown home in the president's own aircraft and, in the dead of night at a deserted airfield near San Francisco, the honor guard who brought Nicholas' body home, with no one there to watch, insisted on performing the full ceremonial due to a national hero. Now streets, schools and squares from the Alps to Sicily, and the largest hospital in Italy, are named for him.

With the worldwide media coverage that followed, people who had scarcely given the subject a thought became aware that thousands of unnecessary deaths result every year from the shortage of donated organs. On his grave one day I found an anonymous note, typical in its intensity. It said simply, "Dear little Nicholas, we love you. God bless you to eternity, sweet child."

In Italy alone, organ donation rates have tripled since he was killed, so that thousands of people are alive who otherwise would have died. Obviously, an increase of that magnitude – not even remotely approached in other developed countries – must have a variety of causes, but it seems clear that Nicholas' story was a catalyst that changed the attitude of an entire nation.

Since then, all seven of his recipients have had new lives. To think of just one of them: Maria Pia, who bounced back to health, married in the full bloom of womanhood and has had two children, a boy and a girl - two whole lives that would never have been. As far as anyone knows, the livers of all three, in a family with a history of liver disease, are working perfectly. And, yes, she named her boy Nicholas.

Organ donation goes beyond even life-saving surgery, however, to another level of understanding. A young woman from Rome wrote this to us: "Since when your son has died, my heart is beating faster. I think that people, common persons, can change the world. When you go to the little graveyard place please say this to him, 'They closed your eyes, but you opened mine.' "

Printed in the United States
121969LV00003B/32/A